THE WI BOOK OF
— OF —
SALSAS
AND
UNUSUAL PRESERVES

GRACE MULLIGAN

WI BOOKS

in association with Stable Ltd
Glebe House, Church Street,
Crediton, Devon EX17 2AF

Illustrated by Michael Lye

British Library Cataloguing in Publication Data.
A CIP catalogue record for this book is available from the British Library.

ISBN 0 947990 52 6

Printed and bound in Great Britain by Short Run Press Ltd, Exeter, Devon

Acknowledgements
The publisher is grateful to Tate & Lyle Sugars for their support for the publication of this book.

The author is also grateful to Dilwen Phillips for editorial help, to Caroline Grace for typing, and to Simon Goodenough of Stable Ltd.

Note
Tests carried out at the Home Preservation section of the Long Ashton Research Station, Bristol, and with WI Markets, in conjunction with Tony D'Angeli in 1992, prove that the eating and keeping quality of preserves is the same when using beet and cane sugar.

CONTENTS

CONTENTS

CONTENTS

INTRODUCTION

In the '70s, long before I had anything to do with the television series, *Farmhouse Kitchen*, I was one of about half a dozen preservers who made some jars of jellies, pickles and relishes to 'go on television'. I don't think we really knew what it was all about but a letter had come from our WI County Federation and we, of course, did not want to let our WI down. We produced a brilliant contribution with perfectly set jelly and precisely positioned labels in wonderfully neat writing. It turned out that our jars were part of the introduction to the programme. While the theme music played and the words "Farmhouse Kitchen" came up on the screen, a large, old-fashioned press (cupboard) slowly opened to reveal our preserves – we were delighted!

By the time I presented the programme, the press was replaced by a lovely rural scene of my producer and director's beautiful farmhouse near the North Yorkshire town of Hawes. Mary and Graham Watts, who were responsible for the programme, persuaded a neighbour with a flock of sheep to get them to amble down the field by the house, and Graham's pyjamas were blowing on the line!

In days gone by, I once read in an old cookery book that the competent and thrifty housewife always had a well-filled stock cupboard with "rows of jars shining like good deeds in a naughty world". Certainly no other branch of cookery gives you the chance for self-satisfaction to contemplate at leisure the work of your hands before it disappears.

Preserves have come a long way and are now part of the equipment of every chef, keen cook and consumer. The shelves of our supermarkets, heritage centres and souvenir shops are stuffed with a dazzling mixture of flavoured vinegars, relishes, herb jellies and conserves – some with unnerving price tags for things you can make yourself for pence. You might find a flavoured vinegar in an elaborately decorative bottle, tied with ribbon and raffia and labelled with exotic lettering.

Try making your own rose petal vinegar. Tightly stuff a jar with clean, highly scented dark rose petals. Crush them a little as you push them in. Top up with white wine vinegar. Leave for a month, then strain off and discard the petals. You now have a lovely flavoured vinegar to use in salad dressings. You could sweeten it slightly to dribble over vanilla ice cream or 'panna cotta' (Italian cream jelly).

There used to be a sort of hierarchy of pickles with walnuts, mushrooms and delicate silver-skin onions at the top end and other types of chutneys and relishes regarded as very coarse fellows! Nowadays all sorts of unusual preserves can be made from our own produce and also from the marvellous selection of exotic fruit and vegetables now available to us. Whereas in the past our year consisted of the frenzy of marmalade making in January, the jam, jelly and conserve season in the summer, and another frenzy of pickles, chutney and so on to use up our surplus apples and green tomatoes, we now have our freezers to spread the load and also the exotic fruit and vegetables arriving all the year round. Our recipes are changing, too, with the spicy accompaniments for Indian food, hot chilli flavours from South America, and pickled mooli (white radish) with Chinese dishes. Our tastes are expanding and changing all the time.

I know that the salsa is a popular dance but it is the salsas of the food world which are the 'in thing' at the moment. Although not a preserve but rather an accompaniment, you can allow your versatility to run wild and experiment as you never have before. It is common now to add two or even three types of salsa to a dish. These can be sweet or savoury and it is often these additions that attract us on a restaurant menu. The golden rules are that the ingredients of a salsa should look fresh and inviting as well as tasting good. Fresh fruit, fresh crisp vegetables, fresh herbs combine in any number of ways to enhance, stimulate and add to the pleasure of what you are eating.

The other accompaniments I have put in cover a wide range of things you might consider adding to your plate to complement or contrast. Texture is important – if you are eating, say, a crisply fried fishcake, a smooth accompaniment like a dollop of mayonnaise flavoured with grain mustard, a shot of lemon juice and a sprinkling of chopped chives would be perfect. A simple starter like a sweet and sour dipping sauce with a few sticks of carrot, peppers and tiny mushrooms could not be easier. If you dislike a communal dip, give everyone a little pot all to themselves – an egg cup would do. Another easy starter I was introduced to in Italy is just a flavoured olive oil and bread. The olive oil can be bought flavoured with herbs, lemons and chilli; each person has a plate with a thin film of oil on it and a basket of warm ciabatta chunks for dipping. You could of course make your own flavoured oil. Stuff in a jar some fresh herbs, chopped garlic, peppercorns, a few slices of lime or lemon or orange. Pour over the oil, cover and leave for a few days. Taste the oil and add anything you think it needs, and leave again. Drain the oil into a bottle with a sprig of rosemary or tarragon in it, and serve. With a glass of red wine, this is the easiest starter I know.

I hope you enjoy this book. Do let me know if you find a winner to suit your family. Whatever you do, just remember you are following a long tradition, and you are helping to keep that custom alive.

JAMS, JELLIES, MARMALADES & CURDS

Nowadays the word 'preserve' means different things to different people. The traditional jams made the old way, with a high proportion of sugar, are true preserves. They were stored in the larder or pantry. Even when opened, I do not remember having to put them in the fridge. I notice that many so-called 'Traditional Commercial Preserves' come with the warning, "once opened store in the fridge". This warning is also put on 'jam' made with a mixture of sugar and apple juice (or other fruit juices) and also on 'jam' which contains no sugar at all, just concentrated sweet fruit juice. Only one manufacturer makes a point of labelling his 'jam' as a natural 'fruit spread' which goes mouldy in three weeks.

The soft set 'conserves' of France, which use less sugar, have a truly wonderful, fresh flavour but are more suited to eating with French bread sticks. A swift scoop is needed to drop the conserve on a small piece of bread and then straight into your mouth. The same can be said of 'freezer jams': they have great flavour but no sticking power. I once watched a man struggling with his cream-tea scones, with jam running everywhere, including down his hands and chin! I discussed this with a young BBC Producer, who was very sniffy about "all that sugar". "I only need one teaspoon of marmalade on my morning toast," I said, "and because it spreads so easily that's all I use." Children also need jam that spreads and stays.

Jams, jellies and marmalades should have a sufficiently high sugar content to prevent fermentation, but they must also, after making, be put into clean jars and covered immediately with either a wax circle or metal twist. Jars should be filled to within 3 mm (¹/₈ inch) of the rim. A cover should be placed on each jar as it is filled.

A good jam should:
- keep well
- be clear and bright
- be characteristic in colour
- be well set, but not too stiff
- have a distinct fruity flavour

Jellies should be bright, clear and sparkling. They are similar to jams in the principle of making, but as only the juice is used (all traces of pulp, skin, pips being removed) considerably more fruit is required than in jam making. Damaged and windfall fruit, providing it is under-ripe, can be used (the damaged parts being cut away). Economical and interesting jellies can be made by using fruits from hedgerows.

It is misleading to give approximate yields for each jelly recipe, as results depend on the type and quality of the fruit used and also on the growing season.

SEVILLE ORANGE CURD
Yield 675 g (1¹/₂ lb)

This delectable recipe came from an article in the *Financial Times* by Phillipa Davenport, which I cut out years ago.

3 Seville oranges (heavy, juicy ones are best)
175 g (6 oz) granulated sugar
3 large size eggs
115 g (4 oz) unsalted butter, cut up small

1. Grate the orange zest into a small saucepan, on the biggest holes in your grater. Add the juice of the oranges, the sugar and the butter. Over a low heat, cook very gently until the butter has melted and the sugar, too.
2. Break the eggs into a biggish heat-proof bowl and whisk lightly until the yolks and whites are well mixed.
3. Pour the hot butter mixture over the eggs in a thin stream while still whisking the eggs at the same time.
4. Strain this mixture through a nylon sieve into a clean heat-proof bowl and set this over a pan of simmering water (or use a double boiler pan if you have one). Cook the curd gently and stir it often. It will take at least 15 minutes to thicken to the consistency of cream.
5. Pour into small warm jars and cover with a waxed disc and cellophane.
6. Store in a fridge or cold larder and eat within 5–6 weeks.

DUTCH ROSIE

This jam recipe came from Holland via a Scottish WRI member, Anne Wallace, who was often a guest on my television series, *Farmhouse Kitchen*. The hips I used were the fruits of a rose called 'Rosa Roseraie De L'Hay'. The bush has unremarkable summer flowers but these wonderful red fat round berries afterwards, which look magnificent against the light green foliage. It is also a very prickly rose and is used quite often as a hedge.

900 g (2 lb) ripe red rose hips (unwrinkled)
1 large grapefruit
1 large sweet orange
4 tbsp fresh lemon juice
granulated sugar
water
muslin or nylon in which to tie the seeds

1. Use a knife to top and tail each rose hip. Cut round the middle of each hip, just enough to cut through the flesh. You can lift the top off like a little hat, and you are left with all the seeds, which have to be removed. This is a tedious job, so ask for help from anyone with nimble fingers. I used a teaspoon to scoop out the seeds, which are firmly attached to a central stalk, which I also scooped out.
2. Prepare the grapefruit and the orange as follows. Cut each fruit into quarters. Use your fingers to find and rescue every seed. Set aside the seeds, tied in the muslin or nylon. Now slice the fruit away from the pith on each quarter. Remove and discard the pith. The easiest way to do this is to lay each quarter, skin down, on the board, and then, using a sawing action with the blade held almost flat, remove the layer of white pith, leaving you with the skin only.
3. Put the red shells of the rose hips in a food processor with the skins of the orange and grapefruit and reduce to crumbs. Put these crumbs in a large, heavy-based saucepan, with the tiny bundle of seeds, and barely cover with water. Set aside overnight if possible.
4. Next day, bring the mixture to a boil, then reduce to a simmer and cook gently until the hips and peels are very soft and you have a thick pulp.
5. Measure this pulp and return it to a clean pan. Add sugar in the usual proportion of 600 ml (1 pint) pulp to 450 g (1 lb) sugar. Stir this into the pulp over a low heat. Once the sugar has dissolved, add the lemon juice and bring the mixture to a brisk boil until setting point is reached.
6. Store the lovely coral-coloured jam in warm jars and seal immediately. Store in the dark to keep the colour bright.

LOW SUGAR NECTARINE (OR PEACH) JAM

Yield 900 g (2 lb)

900 g (2 lb) nectarines (or peaches)
225 g (8 oz) granulated sugar
125 ml (4 fl oz) commercial pectin
30 ml (1 fl oz) fresh lemon juice

1. Peel the fruit by dropping into boiling water. Leave for a few minutes. The skin should slip off easily.
2. Remove the stones and chop the fruit.
3. Put the fruit and lemon juice in a roomy pan and simmer until the fruit is soft – about 15 minutes.
4. Stir in the sugar and, when this has dissolved, bring the heat up to a rolling boil for 7 minutes.
5. Remove the pan from the heat and stir in the pectin.
6. Pot into hot jars and cover.

LEMON & CARROT JAM

Yield 2.25 kg (5 lb)

Surprisingly good!

675 g (1¹/₂ lb) lemons (approx. 4-5 lemons)
450 g (1 lb) fresh juicy carrots
1.7-2.3 litres (3-4 pints) water
1.8 kg (4 lb) granulated sugar, warmed
square muslin or fine net curtaining

1. Scrub the lemons; slice very finely. Remove the pips and set aside. Use scissors to cut each slice into small pieces. Do this over a bowl, to catch any juice.
2. Top, tail and peel the carrots; grate finely on the largest hole on a metal grater.
3. Tie the seeds in a bundle and put with the lemon pieces, carrot and water into a large bowl, and set aside covered overnight.
4. Next day, tip this mixture into a large pan and bring to the boil. Reduce this to a simmer and continue cooking until the mixture has reduced by half – about 45–60 minutes.
5. Stir in the warm sugar, and stir until it has dissolved. Bring to a boil and reduce the heat to a gentle boil until setting point is reached. Stand for 7–8 minutes to allow the peel to settle.
6. Stir again, then put into warm dry jars and cover in the usual way.

CARROT & LEMON JAM

Yield 900 g (2 lb)

This is quite different to the previous recipe for LEMON AND CARROT JAM.

550 g (1 lb 4 oz) fresh young carrots (not woody)
450 g (1 lb) granulated sugar
2 thin-skinned lemons
6 cardamom pods, peeled and split (use seeds only, lightly crushed)

1. Top, tail and peel the carrots. Grate on a metal grater – you need 500 g (1 lb) prepared carrot.
2. Grate the peel from the two lemons and squeeze the juice.
3. Put carrots, lemon zest, juice and sugar and cardamoms in a heavy pan. Stir over a gentle heat until the sugar dissolves, then boil hard until the mixture is very thick.
4. Put into warm jars and cover. Store in the fridge.

PALE GUAVA PRESERVE WITH WALNUTS

Yield 550 g (1¹/₄ lb)

Pot in small jars and serve with a good strong cheese or with cream on warm scones.

2 guavas – about 450 g (1 lb)
350 ml (12 fl oz) water
30 ml (2 tbsp) fresh lemon juice
450 g (1 lb) granulated sugar, warmed
25 g (1 oz) pale good quality walnuts, chopped

1. Top and tail the fruit and peel thinly. Chop into small pieces and put into a pan with the water and lemon juice.
2. Cook gently for about 30 minutes or until the fruit is mushy and the liquid has reduced a little.
3. Then to remove the seeds, push the fruit and the liquid through a nylon sieve.
4. Measure the purée and make it up to 600 ml (1 pint) with water.
5. Put this purée into a deep pan and heat it. Stir in the sugar and stir over a low heat until it is dissolved. Now bring up to a gentle boil, stirring often until the mixture is thick and creamy.
6. Stir in the walnuts and pot and cover in the usual way.

RASPBERRY JAM IN THE MICROWAVE   *Yield 450 g (1 lb)*

This can be unsweetened 'jam' if you wish. Omit artificial liquid sweetener. This is not a true 'preserve' but it has a good fresh taste. Store in the fridge and use up in 7–10 days.

450 g (1 lb) fresh raspberries
1 packet of powdered gelatine
45 ml (3 tbsp) cold water
sugar or artificial liquid sweetener

1. Put the fruit in a large bowl. Cover the bowl loosely with cling film or a plate set at an angle. Cook for a total of 10 minutes on HIGH, stirring after 5 minutes. At this point, the fruit should be soft and pulpy.
2. Scrape down the sides of the bowl and sweeten the fruit to taste with either sugar or liquid sweetener. Stir to encourage the sugar to dissolve.
3. Put the 3 tbsp of cold water into a cup. Sprinkle the gelatine over the surface. Set the cup aside for 4–5 minutes, then cook on HIGH for just 20–25 seconds. Stir to encourage the gelatine to dissolve. Add this mixture to the fruit.
4. Allow the jam to stand for about 5–7 minutes before pouring it into two small warm jars.

NO SUGAR PLUM JELLY

1.3 kg (3 lb) plums, wiped, halved and stoned
50 g (2oz) powdered gelatine
10 ml (2 tsp) artificial liquid sweetener
2–3 drops almond essence
850 ml (1½ pints) water

1. Put the plum halves in a pan with the water. Simmer for about 30 minutes or until the fruit is extremely soft.
2. Strain through a nylon sieve into a clean pan and push some of the pulp through as well. Re-heat this mixture but do not boil, and sprinkle the powdered gelatine into the hot juice about a tablespoonful at a time. Stir to dissolve the gelatine or use a wire whisk. Lift off any scum.
3. Remove the pan from the heat. Strain again if you wish, just in case there are any gelatine 'balls' which have not dissolved.
4. Stir in the artificial sweetener and the almond essence, then pot into small warm jars. Cover in the usual way.

CANADIAN CONSERVE WITH APPLES & CRANBERRIES

Yield 1.8–2.25 kg (4–5 lb)

4 large, hard, eating apples, peeled, cored and chopped
30 ml (2 tbsp) water
15 ml (1 tbsp) granulated sugar
90 ml (6 tbsp) maple syrup
550 g (1¹/₄ lb) cranberries, fresh or frozen
15 ml (1 tbsp) orange peel, cut into small, fine strips (avoid white pith)

1. Put the apples, sugar and water in a large covered pan over a low heat. Shake the pan or stir from time to time to prevent sticking – 5–6 minutes should be enough to soften the apples slightly.
2. Add the maple syrup, cranberries and orange zest. Continue to cook gently with the lid on, stirring from time to time for a further 10 minutes or until the berries have popped and the skins are soft.
3. Spoon into warm clean jars. Cover and cool. Store in the fridge for up to a month.

BLUEBERRY & BRAMLEY JELLY

675 g (1¹/₂ lb) Bramley cooking apples
675 g (1¹/₂ lb) blueberries
1.4 litres (2¹/₂ pints) water
675 g (1¹/₂ lb) granulated sugar

1. Wipe the apples and cut away any bruised patches. Cut into small pieces including skin and cores. Rinse the blueberries in a sieve and shake well. Put both kinds of fruit in a large pan and simmer with the lid on until soft and pulpy. Stir often, mashing down the fruit.
2. Strain this pulp through a jelly bag or a large nylon sieve with a fine mesh. Do not try to hurry this process by squeezing the fruit. Leave the fruit to drip overnight if you can – you should have about 850 ml (1¹/₂ pints) of juice. If you have more than this, put the juice in a clean pan and simmer it to evaporate some of the liquid.
3. Warm the sugar by putting it in the microwave for about 1–1¹/₂ minutes only. Stir the warm sugar into the juice and continue stirring until the sugar has dissolved. Bring up to a gentle boil and test for a set on a cold saucer.
4. Pot and cover into small jars in the usual way.

JELLIED DAMSON & WALNUT PRESERVE

Yield 1.1 kg (2¹/₂ lb)

I first tasted nuts in preserves in France and have loved them ever since. However, do take care to get really top quality walnuts. I find the pale ones taste the best. Nuts should be stored in the fridge or freezer. They go rancid very easily. This recipe came to me from a viewer at the time when we were first able to buy sugar with pectin. I find that the sugar with pectin works better with strongly flavoured fruit.

900 g (2 lb) English damsons
900 g (2 lb) sugar with pectin
1.2 litres (2 pints) water
200 g (7 oz) top quality walnuts, chopped small
   (currant size is about right for me)

1. Rinse the damsons first, drain and put them into a roomy pan and then pour in the 1.2 litres (2 pints) water. Bring to the boil, then reduce to a simmer until the fruit is very soft indeed.
2. Scoop up as many stones as you can prior to the slow business of pushing all the fruit through a nylon sieve. I do this a bit at a time and use a serving spoon to push the fruit back and forward, scraping off the pulp from the underside of the sieve as I go.
3. Pour the pulp and juice into a clean, roomy pan with the sugar. Bring slowly up to boiling point, stirring to dissolve the sugar. Boil hard for just 2-3 minutes.
4. Stir in the walnuts and remove the pan from the heat. Allow the pan to stand for about 5-8 minutes. This standing time makes sure that the walnuts do not float to the surface.
5. Stir again and put into small, warm jars and cover.

QUICK MINT JELLY IN THE MICROWAVE

Make this early in the season when the mint is bright green and full of flavour.

600 ml (1 pint) unsweetened, concentrated apple juice
300 ml ($^{1}/_{2}$ pint) distilled White Malt vinegar
1 kg (1 bag) sugar with pectin
knob of butter
75 ml (5 tbsp) fresh mint, finely chopped (I find this easy with scissors)
2–3 drops green food colour (optional)

1. Put the apple juice and vinegar in a large 2.8 litre (5 pint) bowl. Microwave on HIGH for 10 minutes.
2. Remove the bowl and add in the sugar, gradually stirring all the time. Add the butter, then microwave on HIGH, stirring often for about 10–12 minutes or until the jelly has boiled hard for at least 1 full minute.
3. Remove the bowl from the microwave, stir in the mint and the colouring (if you are using it). Allow the jelly to stand for 30 minutes, but give it a stir every now and then until you can see that the mint is suspended in the jelly and is no longer floating to the surface.
4. Pot into small, warm jars and cover in the usual way.

MAGICAL MEDLAR JELLY

The magical bit about this lovely jelly is that the fruit juice, to start off with, is a dreary brown colour, which turns to deep red when the sugar goes in.

2.7 kg (6 lb) medlars
water
granulated sugar

1. Wash the fruit and cut it up roughly. Barely cover with water and cook gently until very soft. Mash hard during the cooking process.
2. Strain this pulp through a jelly bag or large square of scalded cotton. Resist the temptation to squeeze the pulp, as this makes the juice cloudy. Leave to drip overnight if you can.
3. Measure the juice and weigh out the sugar, using the proportion of 600 ml (1 pint) juice to 450 g (1 lb) sugar.
4. In a clean pan, warm the juice and sugar until the sugar has dissolved. Now bring up to a gentle boil until setting point is reached.

MINT & ELDERBERRY JELLY

I have cooked and tried many elderberry recipes and have never been very pleased with the preserve until I found this one. It was originally written up by Frances Bissel, *The Times* cookery correspondent. This is my own version.

Take care to gather elderberries which are well away from the roadside. To strip the berries, I have found it much easier to use a plastic bucket or a very deep bowl. To pull the berries off the stalks, I use a large, old-fashioned fork with long tynes. Hold the berries well down into the bowl or bucket and force the berries downwards with the fork.

I don't need to tell you that the stain from these dark berries is almost impossible to shift!

450 g (1 lb) cooking apples (under-ripe ones are even better)
1.3 kg (3 lb) elderberries, stripped weight
55 g (2 oz) fresh mint leaves (I prefer the old-fashioned oval-leaf mint, the one
    which gets 'rust' late in the season!)
1.7 litres (3 pints) water
granulated sugar

1. Rinse the apples, then chop roughly – peel, core and all. Put them with the prepared elderberries, water and just half of the mint leaves into a large pan or preserving pan.
2. Cook until the fruit is soft and mushy, using a potato masher to extract as much flavour as possible. Use a jelly bag or a large scalded square of cotton suspended over a bowl (a long-legged kitchen stool turned upside down is ideal). Leave to drip overnight. Because this is a dark jelly, you can give it a good squeeze as well (clear jelly would go cloudy if you did this).
3. Measure the juice and also the sugar. The proportion is 600 ml (1 pint) juice to 450 g (1 lb) sugar. Warm the juice in a clean pan and stir in the sugar.
4. Tie the rest of the mint in a piece of muslin and add that as well.
5. Once the sugar has dissolved, bring up to a gentle boil until setting point is reached.
6. Remove the mint and pour into small, warm jars. Cover and label.

    Note: Jelly is better in small jars, because once the pot is opened the jelly does start to 'weep' a little.

LEMON-SCENTED GERANIUM JELLY

1.3 kg (3 lb) firm red-skinned crab apples	granulated sugar
1.7 litres (3 pints) water	2–3 drops red colouring (optional)
30 ml (2 tbsp) fresh lemon juice	
6–8 scented geranium leaves (the highly perfumed kind), finely chopped	

1. Wash the fruit in cold water and remove any stalks Wipe clean the other end of each apple. Cut out any bruised bits and discard these. Chop the rest roughly, skins, pips, cores and all.
2. Cover the chopped fruit with the water and simmer for about 50–60 minutes or until the fruit is very soft. Mash with a potato masher if the fruit is very hard.
3. Strain the contents of the pan, being very careful to avoid squeezing the pulp. Straining does take time and some people prefer to do it overnight.
4. Measure the juice and add 450 g (1 lb) granulated sugar to 600 ml (1 pint) juice. Stir in the geranium leaves (I snip away the hard centre rib on each leaf). Over a low heat, stir until the sugar has dissolved; boil briskly to setting point.
5. Allow the jelly to cool slightly so the leaves do not float to the surface. Add the red colouring at this point if you wish. Stir again, then pot in the usual way.

TARRAGON & LEMON JELLY

A wonderful accompaniment for hot roast chicken or turkey. Chop the tarragon with scissors if the leaves are big enough. Preserving sugar is much better for jellies, as there is much less froth.

450 g (1 lb) early, hard cooking apples or crab apples
1.3 kg (3 lb) thin-skinned lemons, scrubbed and thinly sliced
3.4 litres (6 pints) water
45 ml (3 large tbsp) fresh tarragon
preserving sugar
knob butter

1. Wipe and chop the apples roughly. Put these and the sliced lemons with all the seeds in a preserving pan, with the water and half of the tarragon. Bring to a boil, then reduce to a simmer for about 1½ hours. The fruit should be very soft.
2. Stir well before turning the pulp into a jelly bag or clean tea towel suspended over a bowl. Leave to drip overnight. Do not squeeze the fruit or your jelly will be cloudy.

3. Measure the juice and weigh out the sugar in the proportion of 600 ml (1 pint) juice to 450 g (1 lb) sugar.
4. In a clean pan, bring the juice to a boil. Reduce to a simmer. Stir in the sugar and keep the heat low until the sugar is dissolved.
5. Add the butter. Bring to a full boil for about 15 minutes.
6. Test for a set. Lift off any surface scum and stir in the rest of the tarragon. Leave the jelly to cool, then stir gently to distribute the tarragon.
7. Put into small jars in the usual way.

LIME & GINGER MARMALADE

Yield 1.1 kg (2¹/₂ lb)

8–10 limes
4 chunks stem ginger in syrup
1.3 kg (3 lb) granulated sugar, warmed
1.4 litres (2¹/₂ pints) water
large square of fine nylon cloth or double muslin

1. Limes are often very hard, so soften by soaking in boiling water, or put them in the microwave for 10–15 seconds. Another method is to freeze them overnight, then defrost, and you will find they are much easier to handle. Pare off the lime skin very finely, using a sharp knife, and shred it and set it aside. Cut the limes in half and squeeze the juice. Scrape out any pulp with a spoon and reserve all the pips (there will not be much pulp).
2. Put the water into a roomy pan and pour in the lime juice and the finely shredded zest plus any pulp. Put the seeds and the remaining shells (chopped up) into a bundle. Tie this tightly and drop into the pan as well. Cover the pan and set it aside overnight. This helps the peel to soften.
3. Next day, slice the ginger into fine slices and then into matchsticks, and add to the pan. Bring the contents up to a boil, then reduce the heat to a steady simmer. Continue cooking until the amount of liquid is reduced by half and the peel is soft and transparent.
4. Stir in the warmed sugar and stir until it is dissolved. Bring up to a steady boil until setting point is reached, when a teaspoon of the mixture will set on a cold plate and wrinkle when pushed.
5. Remove pan from the heat and leave marmalade for about 10 minutes or so. This prevents the peel from floating to the surface. Remove the bag of seeds and pith to a nylon sieve and squeeze out as much juice as possible.
6. Put into warm jars and cover.

MICROWAVE SEVILLE ORANGE MARMALADE

Yield 1.1 kg (2¹/₂ lb)

900 g (2 lb) Seville oranges
2 thin-skinned heavy lemons, juice only
900 (2 lb) granulated sugar, warmed in the oven
knob butter
850 ml (1¹/₂ pints) boiling water

1. Wash and dry the oranges and remove any green stalks. Take a sharp knife and remove the zest as thinly as possible (avoid the white pith). Shred the zest as finely as you can, and set it aside. Slice up the oranges.
2. Put this chopped mixture into a large heat-proof bowl – about 2.8 litres (5 pints) – and pour over the boiling water. Microwave uncovered on HIGH for 15 minutes.
3. Strain this mixture into a big jug, squeeze the pulp hard and then discard it.
4. Pour the hot juice back into the cleaned bowl. Stir in the shredded peel. Microwave on HIGH for 20–25 minutes or until the peel disintegrates when you press it between thumb and forefinger. Stir twice during the cooking of the peel.
5. Stir in the lemon juice and the warm sugar, and continue stirring until the sugar dissolves.
6. Use cling-film to cover the bowl, then microwave again on HIGH for 10 minutes.
7. Stir in the butter; microwave again for 6 minutes, stirring once during cooking.
8. Test for setting point on a cold plate. If the set is soft, microwave for another 30 seconds.
9. Leave the marmalade to cool for 10 minutes, then spoon into warmed jars and cover with screw caps when hot.

Note: The glass bowl will always be extremely hot. Move it with great care.

MISER'S MINCED MARMALADE   *Yield 3.6 kg (8 lb)*

After squeezing fruit juice, save any orange or grapefruit peel in the freezer until you have about 675 g (1½ lb). I also save seeds, since they contribute to the setting quality of any preserve. Slice each 'cup' of peel into three and shave off most of the pith from the sweet oranges and grapefruit. Discard this pith, since its strong flavour will spoil the fresh taste of the marmalade. It is worth noting that thin-skinned lemons are smoother and shinier than others.

675 g (1½ lb) orange & grapefruit peel
450 g (1 lb) whole thin-skinned lemons, scrubbed
4 fresh limes, scrubbed
2.7 kg (6 lb) granulated sugar, warmed
1.7 litres (3 pints) water
circle of muslin or fine mesh curtaining

1. Put the orange and grapefruit peel in a food processor.
2. Top and tail the lemons and slice thickly. Pick out the seeds and set them aside. Add the chopped lemons to the food processor.
3. Peel the rind off the limes. Set this aside. Chop the flesh, pick out and reserve the seeds, and add the flesh only to the food processor, plus 300 ml (10 fl oz) water.
4. Whiz this mixture until it reaches the consistency you like (chunky or fine).
5. Tip this mixture, plus the seeds tied in the muslin, into a pressure cooker if you are in a hurry, and cook at top pressure for 10 minutes.
6.. When it has cooled, tip this mixture into a preserving pan and add the rest of the water – about 1.4 litres (2½ pints).
7. Cut out the pressure cooker bit if you wish and, instead, leave the mixture to soak overnight.
8. Next day, bring the preserving pan mixture to a boil, then down to a simmer. Reduce the volume by about one-third, or until the mixture is a thick mush. Stir often. It is very easy to burn at this point.
9. Stir in the warm sugar. When this has dissolved, bring to a boil then reduce to a gentle boil until setting point is reached.
10. Allow the mixture to stand for about 7 minutes. Then stir again and pot into hot jars and cover.

   Note: 'Setting point' is when a teaspoon of the hot preserve, spooned onto an icy cold plate, forms a skin which will wrinkle when pushed.

SALSAS

Salsas, which came from South America, were originally hot and spicy, with Jalapeño chillies, peppers, tomatoes and onions. In America, salsa is said to be even more popular than Tomato Ketchup. It is easy to understand why this simple accompaniment pleases everyone. It is not difficult to make and it is part sauce, part salad and part relish. You can leave it as chunky as you please or reduce it to a very fine texture. It is not usually cooked, and the fresh fruit, fresh vegetables and herbs look bright and inviting. As always happens, recipes are turning up now with some of the salsa ingredients lightly cooked then cooled, and even sweet salsa can be delicious.

The mixture is usually wet and can be served with grilled or barbecued fish or meat, stirred into soups, pasta, cottage cheese or fromage frais, dolloped on top of a baked potato or used as a party dip. Salsa was never meant to keep well, so most salsas need to be eaten within 2–3 days. The fresh herbs are the things which begin to discolour first.

I think one of the salsa's greatest assets is that you can often avoid making a gravy or sauce. It is also another way of eating part of the five items of fresh fruit and fresh vegetables a day that we are asked to take for the sake of our health.

CORIANDER SALSA

This strongly flavoured salsa is particularly good used as a dip for Naan bread and samosas.

1 bunch fresh coriander
$^1/_4$ fresh green chilli
150 ml (5 fl oz) natural yoghurt

1. Rinse the bundle of coriander under a running tap, then pat dry with kitchen towels. Chop off all the leaves, discarding any which are discoloured. I use the stems as well, as long as they are soft.
2. Chop the $^1/_4$ chilli with scissors into tiny pieces. Keep the rest aside, since you may wish to add more.
3. Put all the ingredients into a blender or a food processor and whiz to a pulp.
4. Taste and adjust the flavour. You may wish to add a touch of sugar as well.
5. Eat within 2–3 days and store in a fridge.

SHARP ANCHOVY SALSA

55 g (2 oz) tin of anchovies in oil
25 g (1 oz) mixed green herbs – chives, basil, parsley
55 g (2 oz) preserved capers, drained and rinsed
1 small clove garlic, peeled and chopped
15 ml (1 tbsp) oil
15 ml (1 tbsp) white wine vinegar
2.5 ml ($^1/_2$ tsp) grain mustard
salt and pepper

1. Rinse and de-bone the anchovies.
2. Put them in a blender (or use a stick blender), along with the herbs and 25 g (1 oz) of the capers. Whiz this to a purée, then stir in the rest of the capers, oil, vinegar and grain mustard.
3. Taste and adjust the seasoning.

GREEN SALSA (1)

1 large bunch parsley, rinsed
1 large bunch mint, rinsed
15 ml (1 tbsp) preserved capers, rinsed and patted dry
5 anchovy fillets, rinsed and de-boned
90 ml (6 tbsp) olive oil (or light olive oil)
15 ml (1 tbsp) white wine vinegar
1 small clove garlic, peeled and roughly chopped
salt and pepper

1. Take the parsley off the stems (soft green stems can be left).
2. Do the same with the mint and put everything into a blender or food processor. Whiz.
3. Taste and adjust the seasoning to your taste.
4. Use within 3–4 days and store in the fridge.

GREEN SALSA (2)

This salsa is different from GREEN SALSA (1), in that there is no parsley to become discoloured in the way that coriander, watercress and avocado also discolour.

1 small clove garlic, peeled and crushed
5 anchovy fillets, rinsed and finely chopped
1 heaped tbsp capers, rinsed
5 ml (1 tsp) grain mustard
30 ml (2 tbsp) olive oil
60 ml (4 tbsp) fresh lemon juice
15 ml (1 heaped tbsp) chopped cucumber
2–3 drops tabasco
salt and pepper

1. Put everything except the cucumber into the processor and whiz to a rough purée.
2. Stir in the cucumber, taste and adjust the seasoning to taste.
3. Use within 3–4 days.

APPLE SALSA

The idea for this recipe came originally from Val Archer's lovely book, *A Basket of Apples*. I found the taste quite delicious but rather hot, so here is my version.

40 g (1$^{1}/_{2}$ oz) fresh mint leaves
25 g (1 oz) fresh coriander leaves and soft stems
2 Granny Smith apples, peeled, cored and chopped roughly
2 fresh limes, juice and grated rind
2 medium cloves garlic, peeled
$^{1}/_{2}$ fresh green chilli, de-seeded and chopped (add more if you wish)
5 ml (1 tsp) caster sugar
45 ml (3 tbsp) light olive oil

1. Rinse the herbs and pat dry with paper towels.
2. Put everything except the oil into the food processor. Aim for a chunky sauce rather than a smooth one.
3. Add the oil a little at a time.
4. Taste and season.
5. Cover and store in the fridge for 6–7 days.

PEAR & PEPPER SALSA

I used fairly firm pears for this recipe, and I liked the texture.

2 firm pears, peeled, cored and finely chopped
50 ml (2 fl oz) lemon juice
1 small onion (golf ball size), peeled and very finely sliced
1 small yellow pepper, de-seeded and cut into fine strips
10 ml (2 tsp) preserved green peppercorns in brine, drained
30 ml (2 tbsp) fresh coriander leaves and soft stems, chopped

1. Drop the chopped pears into the lemon juice – to stop them going brown.
2. Stir in everything else.
3. Taste and adjust seasoning.
4. Chill for a couple of hours.
5. Use within 2 days.

SALSA VERDE

Green salsa can be a mixture of whichever herbs you wish.

2 fat cloves garlic, peeled and roughly chopped
a good bunch each of parsley, basil and mint
30 ml (2 tbsp) drained capers
15 ml (1 tbsp) Dijon mustard
15 ml (1 tbsp) white wine vinegar
150 ml (5 fl oz) green olive oil

1. Put all the ingredients except the oil into a food processor. Whiz until evenly chopped.
2. Add the oil and whiz again.
3. Serve on the day it is made, since the green colour deteriorates after about 4 hours.

TOMATO SALAD SALSA

45 ml (3 tbsp) freshly chopped coriander leaves and soft stalks
4 large pieces sun dried tomato, drained
50 ml (2 fl oz) lime juice
$^1/_2$ green chilli, de-seeded
4 spring onions, chopped

1. Put everything in the food processor and whiz until fairly smooth.
2. Store in a fridge and eat within 2 days.

MANGO SALAD SALSA

The pretty colour of this salsa is as good as its flavour.

90 ml (6 tbsp) finely chopped fresh mango
30 ml (2 tbsp) pickled ginger, cut into fine strips
10 ml (2 tsp) fresh lemon juice
10 ml (2 tsp) fresh coriander leaves, chopped

1. Stir all the ingredients together. Taste and adjust the seasoning.
2. Store in a fridge and eat within 2 days.

CARIBE SALSA

This idea came from a Sainsbury's leaflet, which I tried and it was lovely – not too hot.

2 Caribe chillies (yellow, sweet and mild)
1 very small onion, peeled and roughly chopped
5 ml (1 tsp) ground cumin
1 fresh medium-sized tomato
1 small clove garlic, peeled
5 ml (1 tsp) salt

1. Halve and de-seed the chillies, then set them on a baking sheet for 15 minutes in a hottish oven (400°F, 200°C, Gas 6).
2. Halve the tomato, then set under a hot grill, with the cut side downwards, until the skin starts to blacken.
3. Remove the tomato and skin, then put all the ingredients in a food processor until smoothish.
4. Cook the mixture in a pan over a moderate heat for about 5 minutes.
5. Cool and serve.

CRANBERRY SWEET & SOUR SALSA

175 g (6 oz) fresh or frozen cranberries
55 g (2 oz) red onion, peeled and chopped
115 g (4 oz) green pepper, de-seeded and chopped
5 ml (1 tsp) finely chopped fresh ginger
45 ml (3 tbsp) oil
85 g (3 oz) pineapple pieces, cut small
1 small fresh tomato, peeled, de-seeded and chopped

1. Stir together the cranberries, onion, pepper, sugar and ginger.
2. Heat the oil in a pan, and turn the cranberry mixture into this. Turn the heat low, and gently cook the mixture, stirring it frequently.
3. When the cranberries are just starting to pop, stir in the pineapple and the tomato, and remove from the heat.
4. Pour away any excess liquid, and serve warm or cold. Wonderful with roasted pork spare ribs..

BLACK BEAN SALSA

I had this Salsa with cold salmon at a party, and it was surprisingly good and unusual.

115 g (4 oz) dried black beans (or use canned beans)
350 g (12 oz) firm red tomatoes, skinned, then cut in half and de-seeded
1 small red chilli, de-seeded and finely chopped
30 ml (2 tbsp) fresh coriander, rinsed and chopped
1 small red onion, peeled and finely chopped
15 ml (1 tbsp) red wine vinegar
15 ml (1 tbsp) olive oil
fat pinch sugar
2.5 ml ($^{1}/_{2}$ tsp) grain mustard
salt and pepper

1. Soak the dried black beans overnight, then rinse and boil hard for 10 minutes, then simmer for 30 minutes until soft. Put in a roomy bowl.
2. Chop the tomato flesh finely, and add this and everything else to the bowl. Stir well.
3. Set aside for the flavour to develop for at least 1 hour. Taste and adjust the seasoning.
4. Store in a fridge and eat within 4 days.

THREE C'S SALSA (CUCUMBER, CARROT & CHILLI)

This salsa is unusual, since it is sweetened, so store it in the fridge and eat within 2 days.

5 ml (1 tsp) honey
30 ml (2 tbsp) hot water
5 cm (2 ins) cucumber, wiped and diced
115 g (4 oz) carrot, peeled and grated
$^{1}/_{2}$ fresh green chilli, de-seeded and finely chopped
2 small shallots, peeled and cut into wafer-thin rings
salt and pepper

1. Melt the honey in the hot water and leave this aside to go cold.
2. Mix all the ingredients and pour over the dressing. Taste and adjust the seasoning. Add more chilli pepper if you wish.

MUSTARD & MINT SALSA

Serve this with very sweet melon sliced thinly as a starter.

60 ml (4 tbsp) olive oil
juice of 1 lemon – 45 ml (3 tbsp)
5 ml (1 heaped tsp) grain mustard
10–15 ml (2–3 tsp) caster sugar
15 ml (1 heaped tbsp) chopped fresh mint leaves

1. Whisk all the ingredients together, and just before serving stir in the chopped mint.
2. Eat on the day it is made. Mint goes very dark very quickly.

GUACAMOLE SALSA

This is almost always served like a paté or as a dip with corn chips and crudités. However, it makes a good salsa-type dressing for fish. Because avocado goes very dark very quickly, it is best to make this just one hour before you need it.

6 large ripe avocados (the pointed end should give when pressed)
2 cloves garlic, peeled and crushed
juice of 2 fresh limes – 45–60 ml (3–4 tbsp)
1 very small hot red chilli, deseeded and finely chopped
2 red tomatoes (skinned and the insides removed), chopped
small wedges of fresh lime
salt and pepper
fresh chopped coriander, to serve

1. Cut each avocado in two, and twist apart. Remove the stone and set this aside. Scrape out the flesh, including the darker green flesh next to the skin.
2. Combine all the other ingredients with the avocado, except the lime wedges. Some people like it chunky and use just a fork; others like it more smooth and use a stick blender.
3. Sprinkle over with the chopped coriander and serve with a wedge of fresh lime.
4. Use immediately. Avocado discolours quickly.

CHUTNEY SALSA

This salsa is unusual in that it is cooked and its base is fresh tomatoes. The chilli flavouring is hot.

30 ml (2 tbsp) vegetable oil
5 ml (1 tsp) each: fennel seeds, cumin seeds, black mustard seeds
1 small knob fresh ginger, peeled and sliced and cut into fine strips
3 cloves garlic, peeled and crushed, with a little salt
450 g (1 lb) fresh ripe tomatoes, peeled and chopped
85 g (3 oz) granulated sugar
2 small green chillies, sliced finely
15 ml (1 tbsp) wine vinegar
85 g (3 oz) plump, ready-to-eat apricots, cut small

1. First heat the oil and fry the fennel, cumin and black mustard seeds briefly.
2. Add the ginger and garlic and stir fry for just a few seconds.
3. Stir in the tomatoes, salt and sugar, and cook gently for about 15 minutes or until the mixture has thickened.
4. Add the chillies, vinegar and apricots, and cook for a further 15 minutes.
5. Spoon into warm vinegar-proof jars, and store in the fridge for up to 10 days.

SRI LANKAN SALSA

large handful fresh mint, leaves and some soft stems
zest and juice of 1 lime
5 ml (1 level tsp) sugar
5 ml (1 level tsp) salt
1 small green chilli, de-seeded and chopped
2 large cloves garlic, peeled and chopped
15 ml (1 heaped tbsp) desiccated coconut, lightly toasted under a grill
2 shallots, peeled and finely chopped
2 large, hard carrots, peeled and grated

1. Into a food processor, put the mint, zest and juice of lime, sugar, salt, green chilli, garlic and coconut. Whiz to a paste (or pulverise in a large mortar).
2. Stir this paste together with the shallots and carrots. Add a splash of water if the salsa is too stiff.
3. Store in the fridge and eat within 2 days.

STRAWBERRY SALSA

This idea came from Polly Brown, a fellow food writer at the *Yorkshire Post*. It looks as good as it tastes, and Polly suggests it would make a good summer starter, too.

175 g (6 oz) ripe but firm strawberries (small ones if possible)
5 cm (2 ins) piece of cucumber, cut into small dice or long strips
    (leave the skin on)
15 ml (1 tbsp) balsamic vinegar

1. Mix the fruit and cucumber.
2. Dribble the vinegar over at the last minute.
3. Eat immediately.

BEEF TOMATO SALSA

2 large beef tomatoes, very ripe but firm
juice from 2 limes – 60 ml (4 tbsp)
5 ml (1 tsp) fresh thyme leaves
salt and black pepper

1. Peel, de-seed and finely chop the tomatoes.
2. Mix all the ingredients together and taste.
3. A pinch or two of caster sugar may be added if the tomatoes are not quite as sweet as they should be.

SOUR CREAM SALSA

175 g (6 oz) cooked chick peas
1 level coffeespoon paprika pepper (or $^{1}/_{4}$ level tsp)
30–45 ml (2–3 tbsp) sour cream
15 ml (1 tbsp) fresh parsley, chopped
2.5 cm (1 inch) fresh cucumber, chopped small
salt and ground pepper

1. Stir all the ingredients together and season to taste.
2. Store in the fridge and eat within 2 days.

YOGHURT & CUCUMBER SALSA

$^1/_2$ a firm cucumber, peeled and chopped
300 ml (10 fl oz) Greek sheep's yoghurt
1 small clove garlic, peeled and crushed, with a little salt
salt and pepper
3 large sprigs of fresh mint
15 ml (1 tbsp) olive oil

1. Strip the mint leaves off the sprigs. Rinse and chop quite small.
2. Stir everything together and season to taste.

WARM SALSA

1 small pepper (red or yellow) or $^1/_2$ red and $^1/_2$ yellow
1 firm red tomato
1 small clove garlic
$^1/_2$ fresh green chilli
1 small shallot
$^1/_2$ firm courgette
30 ml (2 tbsp) vegetable oil
rind and juice of one lemon
dash of olive oil
salt and pepper

1. Grill the pepper halves, skin side up, until they become blackened in patches. Leave them to cool, then skin and de-seed and cut into small squares.
2. Skin the tomato and de-seed.
3. Chop the flesh, de-seed the chilli and chop it finely (I use scissors).
4. Peel and chop the shallot very finely.
5. Trim and dice the courgette as well.
6. Peel and crush the garlic with a little salt.
7. Heat the oil in a small frying pan, then add the chilli, garlic and the shallot. Fry gently until the shallot begins to soften, and then add the chopped courgette. Barely heat the courgettes, then remove the pan from the hob.
8. Stir in the lemon rind and juice, tomato dice, the chopped pepper, and a tiny amount of olive oil. Mix gently and serve.

AVOCADO & CORIANDER SALSA

1 ripe avocado, peeled, cut in half and stoned
30 ml (2 tbsp) freshly chopped coriander
15 ml (1 tbsp) red finely chopped onion
2 medium size, ripe but firm tomatoes
2.5 cm (1 inch) cucumber
30 ml (2 tbsp) lime juice
salt and pepper

1. Chop the avocado, onion and cucumber in smallish pieces. Stir in the lime juice quickly, to prevent the avocado from discolouring.
2. Peel the tomatoes by pouring boiling water over them, then dunking them in cold water one at a time. Cut each tomato in two and discard the insides. Chop the flesh only, then stir into the avocado mixture, followed by the coriander leaves.
3. Stir gently and season to taste.
4. Eat on the day it is made.

CHARRED PEPPER SALSA

Charring or roasting enhances the flavour of peppers in an amazing way. Long, narrow peppers grill more easily than short, fat ones.

3 small peppers, 1 red, 1 yellow, 1 green
1 clove garlic
salt to taste
5 ml (1 tsp) white wine vinegar
15 ml (1 tbsp) olive oil
a few black olives

1. Rinse and dry the peppers and cut off any stems, and halve them from top to bottom, and de-seed. Heat the grill, and set the pepper halves skin side up to the heat. Grill until the skin is charred in places.
2. Remove from the heat and set aside. When cool enough to handle, peel off the skin and any charred bits which stick. Cut the peppers into long strips – not too thin.
3. Very finely chop the peeled garlic and add this to the bowl of peppers, along with salt to taste, wine vinegar and oil.
4. Leave the mixture to absorb the flavour, then serve with the olives.

WHITE CABBAGE SALSA

This salsa is much better if you can set the cabbage aside for the full 3–4 hours. The cabbage goes soft and absorbs the dressing.

$^1/_2$ **small white cabbage**
2.5 ml ($^1/_2$ tsp) salt
30 ml (2 tbsp) fresh lemon juice
10–15 ml (2–3 tsp) olive oil
5 ml (1 tsp) dried mint, crushed

1. Shred the cabbage as finely as you can, and put it in a colander. Sprinkle some salt over the top and turn the cabbage so that the salt reaches all of the cabbage. Put a heavy plate on top, which fits inside the colander, and set aside for 3–4 hours. A great deal of liquid will come out.
2. Squeeze the cabbage with your hands to remove even more liquid, and set in a bowl.
3. Dress it with the lemon juice and oil. Mix well, then add the crushed mint.

ORANGE, FENNEL & WATERCRESS SALSA

2 juicy oranges
$^1/_2$ **small head fennel**
1 small bunch watercress, washed and any limp or yellow leaves removed
tiny dash of nut oil (hazelnut or walnut) or olive oil
salt and pepper

1. Peel the orange like an apple, removing every bit of pith. Now remove the orange segments, using a sharp knife. Hold the orange in your hand over a bowl and cut down between the layers of white pith to release a segment of orange. This is very much easier than it sounds but your knife must be sharp. Chop the segments into 2–3 pieces and place in a bowl.
2. Remove the outer tough layers of fennel, then cut the rest into very thin slivers. Add to the oranges.
3. Chop the watercress into pieces and stir into the orange and fennel mix.
4. Now drizzle the salsa with oil and the juice from half of the second orange.
5. Season to taste.
6. Eat on the same day.

SPICED BANANA SALSA

25 g (1 oz) butter
2.5 ml (^{1}/2 tsp) cumin seed
knife tip of chilli powder (less than a pinch)
1 firm banana, peeled and cut into 1 cm (^{1}/2 inch) slices
15 ml (1 tbsp) grated carrot
1 small, firm tomato, skinned, de-seeded and chopped
olive oil

1. Melt the butter and fry the cumin seed and chilli powder for a minute or so, then add the banana slices. Fry gently, turning the slices over and over. Do not let them go soft.
2. Leave the slices to cool, then stir them into the carrot and tomato, and dribble over a small amount of oil.
3. Adjust chilli to taste but do not overpower the banana.

BEANSPROUTS & HOT PEANUT SAUCE SALSA

large handful of fresh beansprouts
15 ml (1 large tbsp) crunchy peanut butter
15 ml (1 tbsp) single cream (plus extra)
1 large salad onion – white only, wafer thin slices
chilli sauce
pinch of sugar

1. Rinse beansprouts and cut roughly and place in a bowl.
2. Make up a runny sauce by thinning the peanut butter with a little single cream.
3. Add a tiny drop of chilli sauce plus the salad onion and sugar. Stir together and taste, and adjust the seasoning.
4. Dribble this sauce over the beansprouts – you may not need all of it.

AVOCADO & GINGER SALSA

The idea of putting stem ginger with avocado came from the TV cook, Tessa Bramley.

1 small shallot or onion, peeled and chopped small
1 small clove garlic, peeled and crushed with salt
15 ml (1 tbsp) olive oil
2 salad onions
1 lime (or lemon)
1 not-too-large ripe avocado (firm but ripe)
1 small red chilli
1 large firm tomato
1 good chunk of preserved stem ginger
2 pinches sugar
15 ml (1 tbsp) walnut oil
10 ml (2 tsp) of chopped fresh chives
a few sprigs of fresh coriander
salt and pepper

1. In a small pan, heat the olive oil and fry the shallot and garlic until soft but not brown. Set this aside.
2. Top and tail and chop the salad onions finely and on a slant if you can.
3. Grate the zest off the lime (or lemon) and squeeze the juice.
4. Peel, stone and chop the avocado, and put it in a roomy bowl with the lime juice and zest. Stir this round, so that the avocado will not go brown.
5. De-seed the chilli, remove the seeds and snip the flesh into tiny pieces (I use scissors).
6. Peel and de-seed the tomato and chop the flesh.
7. Finely chop the preserved ginger.
8. Stir all the ingredients together in the bowl with the avocado.
9. Add a small spoon of walnut oil, the sugar and chives.
10. Season well and serve with a leaf or two of coriander on top.
11. Eat the same day.

CORIANDER & CUMIN SALSA

15 ml (1 heaped tbsp) chopped fresh coriander
175 g (6 oz) chopped cooked chick peas
1 level saltspoon of ground cumin
knife end of turmeric powder
30 ml (2 tbsp) olive oil
salt and freshly ground pepper

1. Mix all the ingredients together
2. Season to taste.
3. Eat on the same day.

TABBOULEH – PARSLEY & MINT (A TYPE OF SALSA)

1 cup of cold water
55 g (2 oz) cracked wheat or bulgar
30 ml (2 tbsp) fresh lemon juice
30 ml (2 tbsp) olive oil
140 g (5 oz) flat parsley
40 g (1$^{1}/_{2}$ oz) fresh mint leaves
15 ml (1 tbsp) finely chopped onion
1 large tomato, peeled, de-seeded and diced

1. Pour cold water over the cracked wheat and set this aside for about 15 minutes. Strain off the water in a nylon sieve and squeeze the wheat hard.
2. Tip the wheat into a bowl and pour over the lemon juice and olive oil. Stir well and leave this to soak while you prepare the fresh parsley and mint leaves.
3. Stuff these into your food processor and chop down a bit. Do not go too far and produce a purée.
4. Stir the fresh chopped herbs into the cracked wheat, along with the onion.
5. Season with salt and pepper.
6. Serve this vivid green dressing with a border of the chopped fresh tomatoes. It is absolutely delicious with hot grilled food.
7. Eat on the day it is made.

RELISHES

Flavourful relishes, like chutneys, are based on fruit and/or vegetables. They usually contain sugar and vinegar but not in large enough quantities to preserve the ingredients for as long as most other pickles. The method of preparation of relishes is such that the vegetables retain some of their crispness, through little or no cooking.

Relishes add zest to hot or cold dishes, curried and savoury snacks. As with most other cooking, home-made relishes can be far superior to proprietary brands. Sweet and mild, hot or spicy, they can be stirred into casseroles, added to sandwiches, or served with cold cuts. Less well-known spices like star anise, coriander seed and chilli will add a new twist to your recipes, and I have tried to use these in the following recipes.

Because the quantity of vinegar is low, relishes are not true preserves. They can be eaten immediately and most should not be kept longer than 6–8 weeks.

CUCUMBER RELISH   *Serves 8*

1 large, firm cucumber, wiped, topped and tailed and finely diced
15 ml (1 large tbsp) finely chopped onion
45 ml (3 tbsp) olive oil
30 ml (2 tbsp) white wine vinegar
1 fresh chilli, deseeded – red if possible (more if you wish)
2 large fresh and firm tomatoes
salt and pepper

1. Put the cucumber, onion and chilli in a plastic strainer or colander and sprinkle with salt.
2. Set this aside for about half an hour, and give it a stir to allow some of the juices to drain away.
3. Rinse briefly with cold water and shake well. Turn into a big bowl and pour over it the oil and vinegar.
4. Peel the tomatoes and remove the seeds and pith. Chop the flesh and stir this into the cucumber mixture.
5. Season to taste.

SPICED ONION & CRANBERRY RELISH

Yield 1.1 kg (2¹/2 lb)

This relish is flavoured with cardamom, which I enjoyed, but the colour of the cranberries is rather lost, hence the addition of 55 g (2 oz) of the cranberries near the end of cooking, to add some colour, plus a sharp note.

25 g (1 oz) butter
15 ml (1 tbsp) vegetable oil
900 g (2 lb) onions, peeled and chopped small
55 g (2 oz) sugar
spices: 3 cloves
        4 cardamoms, peeled and seeds crushed
        5 peppercorns
square of fine nylon netting or cotton to make a bundle with the spices
2.5 ml (¹/2 tsp) salt
225 g (8 oz) cranberries (fresh or frozen)
juice and zest of 1 large orange
150 ml (5 fl oz) red wine vinegar

1. Fry the chopped onions in the butter and oil until soft. Try not to allow the onions to colour.
2. Add the sugar, then the spices tied tightly into a small bundle.
3. Weigh out and stir in 175 g (6 oz) cranberries, reserving the other 55 g (2 oz).
4. Add the juice and zest of the orange plus the wine vinegar.
5. Cook this mixture covered for about 15 minutes, then take the lid off to allow the liquid to evaporate a bit. Simmer and stir often for about 25 minutes.
6. Add the last of the cranberries about 5 minutes before end of cooking time.
7. Remove and discard the spices. The mixture should be thickish.
8. Pour into warm jars and cover. Store in the fridge.

ROSY RELISH

225 g (8 oz) ripe tomatoes, peeled
115 g (4 oz) onions, peeled and chopped very finely
225 g (8 oz) sharp apples, peeled and chopped
115 g (4 oz) celery, cut small
75 ml (5 tbsp) red pepper, de-seeded and cut small
350 ml (12 fl oz) white vinegar
275 g (9¹/₂ oz) granulated sugar
15 ml (1 tbsp) salt

Spices to be tied in a loose cotton bundle
7.5 cm (3 ins) stick of cinnamon, broken up
8 whole cloves
30 ml (2 tbsp) mustard seed

1. Cut the peeled tomatoes in two and scoop out and discard the insides. Chop the flesh quite small.
2. Put all the ingredients together in a roomy uncovered pan. Add the spice bundle and bring to a boil. Reduce immediately to a simmer for about 30 minutes, or until the onions and apples are soft and the mixture is thick.
3. Discard the spice bag.
4. Pot into warm, clean jars and cover with vinegar proof lids.

MINT & CORIANDER FRESH RELISH

This is an excellent dip for poppadoms or naan bread, or an accompaniment to a rice dish.

150 ml (5 fl oz) natural yoghurt
150 ml (5 fl oz) thick Greek yoghurt
45 ml (3 tbsp) mint leaves, rinsed and chopped
60 ml (4 tbsp) fresh coriander, rinsed and chopped
15 ml (1 tbsp) finely chopped onion
2.5 ml (¹/₂ tsp) salt
1 cm (¹/₂ inch) fresh ginger, finely chopped

1. Stir together the yoghurts, then add everything else.
2. Set aside for the flavours to meld.

SAUCY BEETROOT

Yield 2.25 kg (5 lb)

This is a recipe from Wendy Shand, from my local WI Market. It is a bit like Piccalilli. The beetroot is in a sauce, so should be kept in the fridge. Very good with ham, pork and lamb chops.

12 medium sized beetroot, washed, cooked, cooled, skinned and chopped into dice
   (I do mine in my pressure cooker)
600 ml (20 fl oz / 1 pint) malt vinegar
5 ml (1 heaped tsp) dry mustard
225 ml (8 fl oz) water
310 g (11 oz) granulated sugar
5 ml (1 tsp) white mustard seed
5 ml (1 tsp) salt
30 ml (2 tbsp) flour or cornflour

1. Put the malt vinegar in a jug and sprinkle the flour (or cornflour) and dry mustard over the surface. Whisk this hard to disperse any dry flour.
2. When the liquid is smooth, pour into a large pan with the 225 ml (8 fl oz) water. Bring to a boil, then reduce to a simmer until thickened.
3. Keep whisking so that the sauce is smooth, then add the sugar and the mustard seed. The finished sauce should be the consistency of thick custard.
4. Stir in the chopped beetroot. Return to the boil, then remove from the heat.
5. Pot into warm jars. Cover and cool.

NO-COOK ONION RELISH

1 large Spanish onion, peeled and sliced thinly into rings
50 ml (2 fl oz) fresh lemon juice
5 ml (1 tsp) caster sugar
5 very firm tiny tomatoes, quartered
$^1/_2$ green chilli, de-seeded and finely chopped
5 ml (1 tsp) commercial mint sauce
15 ml (1 tbsp) freshly chopped coriander leaves
salt

1. Into a large bowl, drop the onion rings and add everything else. Stir well.
2. Set aside overnight.
3. Use within 5–6 days. Store in a fridge.

RED & YELLOW & GREEN RELISH

Yield 1.3 kg (3 lb)

This recipe came from Carol Gilling, who sells it at Selby WI Market. It has a wonderful colour and texture.

675 g (1¹/₂ lb) frozen sweetcorn kernels
4 peppers (2 green and 2 red)
600 ml (20 fl oz / 1 pint) white malt vinegar
2 medium sized onions, peeled and cut very small
225 g (8 oz) granulated sugar
10 ml (2 heaped tsp) plain flour
10 ml (2 tsp) dry mustard
5 ml (1 tsp) turmeric powder

1. De-seed and chop the peppers into small strips or squares.
2. Put the sugar, onions, sweetcorn and peppers into a large pan and pour in about half of the vinegar. Bring to a boil.
3. Use the rest of the vinegar to make a thick paste with the flour, turmeric and mustard. Stir a little vinegar into the dry ingredients. When this is smooth, pour in the rest of the vinegar, plus a little of the hot vinegar from the pan.
4. Now tip all of this back over the vegetables and cook gently until the mixture thickens – about 20–25 minutes. Stir often to prevent sticking.
5. Put into warm jars with vinegar proof lids.
6. This relish can be eaten at once but is at its best if left for a few days to mellow.

COCONUT SAMBAL

Serves 4–6

A sambal is the Indonesian word for a relish. Chilli features in most sambals, so be wary of the amount you add, unless you really like hot relishes.

115 g (4 oz) freshly grated coconut
55 g (2 oz) red onion, finely chopped
¹/₂ fresh green chilli. de-seeded and finely chopped
50 ml (2 fl oz) lime juice
1.25 ml (¹/₄ tsp) salt

1. Mix all the ingredients together.
2. Store in the fridge and serve chilled.

PEACH RELISH

This is an ideal recipe for peaches which refuse to ripen.

6 medium sized peaches, fairly firm
60 ml (4 tbsp) caster sugar
60 ml (4 tbsp) cider vinegar
55 g (2 oz) red pepper, de-seeded and chopped into dice
55 g (2 oz) yellow pepper, de-seeded and chopped into dice
^{1}/$_{2}$ fresh green chilli, de-seeded and finely chopped
1 cm (^{1}/$_{2}$ inch) knob fresh ginger, peeled and grated

1. Drop the peaches into boiling water for a few minutes, when the skins should slip off. Peel them if they refuse. Cut each peach right round the middle to the stone. Exert pressure and twist the two halves in opposite directions. Remove the stone and chop the flesh. Discard the stone.
2. Now stir the caster sugar into the vinegar over a low heat. When it has dissolved, bring the heat up again and simmer for a couple of minutes.
3. Drop the chopped peaches into the hot vinegar, along with the peppers and the chilli. Cook gently until the peaches are soft.
4. Set aside to cool, then pour into warm jars and cover.
5. Store in a fridge for up to two weeks.

FRESH RED PEPPER RELISH

Serves 4–6

15 ml (1 tbsp) olive oil
2 medium sized red peppers, de-seeded and cut into strips
2 medium tomatoes, peeled and de-seeded
1 fat clove garlic, peeled and crushed
3 anchovy fillets, rinsed and chopped
45 ml (3 tbsp) balsamic vinegar
salt and pepper

1. Heat oil in a large frying pan (with a lid) and lightly brown the pepper strips.
2. Add tomatoes, garlic and anchovies. Cook gently with the lid on for about 20 minutes, or until the peppers are soft. Cool and whiz to a rough purée.
3. Stir in the balsamic vinegar and season to taste.
4. Store in the fridge and eat within a week.

Note: This is an excellent accompaniment to grilled or fried fish.

CUCUMBER & VINEGAR RELISH

Serves 4

¹/₂ a small firm cucumber
salt
15 ml (1 tbsp) cider vinegar
¹/₂ clove garlic, peeled
10 ml (2 tsp) olive oil
10 ml (2 tsp) white wine vinegar
15 ml (1 tbsp) vegetable oil
2 pinches sugar
pepper

1. Wipe the cucumber and cut in two lengthways. Scoop out the seeds down the middle with a teaspoon. Lean hard on the spoon and drag it along at the same time.
2. Cut the remaining cucumber into thin half-moon slices and put the slices in a colander and then sprinkle with salt all over.
3. Turn the cucumber over and over and leave for about 10–15 minutes until the juices drip out.
4. Now crush the little piece of garlic with salt and mix it into the olive oil with the cider vinegar, vegetable oil and sugar. Season with a tiny amount of salt and pepper.
5. Put the colander with the cucumber under the cold tap to rinse off the salt, squeezing it as far as possible. Turn the pieces out onto a couple of layers of kitchen paper and mop it as dry as possible.
6. Set the cucumber in a bowl and stir in the garlic and oil dressing.
7. Season to taste and chill.
8. Store for up to 2 days.

SWEET PEPPER RELISH

Serves 4

3 small peppers, one red, one yellow, one orange
1 small clove garlic, peeled and crushed with salt
1 small onion, peeled and finely chopped
dash olive oil
15 ml (1 tbsp) granulated sugar
15 ml (1 tbsp) white wine vinegar
4 green cardamoms, skins removed and seeds crushed with a pestle and mortar
knife tip of hot chilli sauce
salt and freshly ground pepper

1. Cut each pepper in two (top to bottom), remove stalk and seeds.
2. Heat the grill and set the pepper halves in the grill pan, skin side up. Keep an eye on the peppers, and when they are scorched in places and going soft remove them.
3. When cool, take off the skin and chop the flesh into neat pieces.
4. Use a frying pan big enough to take all the ingredients. Start by frying the onion and garlic until they are soft but not browned.
5. Stir in the peppers, cardamoms, wine vinegar, sugar and chilli. Simmer gently for about 15–20 minutes, until everything is soft. Try not to stir it too vigorously, or it will turn into mush.
6. Season with salt and pepper.
7. Store in a fridge and use within 3 days.

DRIED FRUIT & MUSTARD RELISH   *Serves 6*

This relish is roughly based on a popular Italian preserve which I have often tasted and found to be rather sweet, so I have adjusted it in the following manner:

10 ml (2 heaped tsp) dry mustard
30 ml (2 tbsp) orange juice
150 ml (5 fl oz) water
dash of white wine vinegar
12 dried, soft apricots, each cut in 2–3 pieces
12 prunes (I used tinned ones because they are nice and small)
30 ml (2 tbsp) raisins
30 ml (2 tbsp) golden sultanas

1. Stone the prunes and set them aside.
2. Put the apricots, raisins and sultanas in a bowl.
3. Mix a little orange juice into the mustard, and when it is smooth add the rest of the juice plus the water and the splash of white wine vinegar.
4. Pour this liquid over the apricots, raisins and sultanas and leave to soak overnight if possible.
5. Next day, simmer this mixture until the fruit is plumped up and the liquid has reduced a bit.
6. Gently stir in the prunes.
7. Set aside to cool. Pot and store in the fridge.
8. Serve with cold duck or pheasant, or hot with roast pork.

BLACKSTRAP RELISH

Yield 1.8 kg (4 lb)

2 large onions (approx total 450 g (1 lb) peeled)
450 g (1 lb) stoned dates, cut small
14 large ripe bananas
1 litre (1^1/$_2$ pints) white wine vinegar
225 g (8 oz) crystallized ginger, chopped small
15 ml (1 tbsp) salt
15 ml (1 tbsp) mixed pickling spice
1 small tin black treacle (454 g)
square of fine mesh nylon curtain fabric or muslin

1. Finely mince or chop the onions.
2. Cut the bananas in long strips and then into pea-sized chunks.
3. Into a large pan, put the onions, dates and bananas. Add about 600 ml (1 pint) vinegar.
4. Tie the pickling spices in a bundle in the net or the muslin. Drop this into the pan followed by the salt. Bring to a gentle boil and stir well for about 5 minutes.
5. Now stir in the rest of the wine vinegar and the black treacle (sometimes called 'Blackstrap'). Continue to cook over a gentle heat until some of the liquid has evaporated and the mixture is thick.
6. Discard the spice bundle and pot into hot jars. Cover with vinegar proof lids.

FRESH MANGO RELISH

This is a recipe originally written in 1986 by the late lamented Jane Grigson.
I have changed it very slightly.

2 large mangoes (not too soft), about 450 g (1 lb) each
15 ml (1 tbsp) finely chopped fresh coconut
30 ml (2 tbsp) finely chopped fresh coriander
15 ml (1 tbsp) finely chopped fresh ginger root
15 ml (1 tbsp) salt
2–3 drops tabasco

If you have no fresh coconut, you can substitute dried coconut. To soften it, just steep it in boiling water for about 10 minutes, then squeeze it dry again.

1. Peel and cut the mango flesh into 1 cm (^{1}/$_2$ inch) cubes. Discard skin and stone.
2. Stir all the ingredients together, and serve as soon as possible

FRESH MINT & MOOLI RELISH

This uncooked relish is delicious but the colour does deteriorate quickly, so eat it up within 4 days.

large bunch fresh mint
115 g (4 oz) white radish (mooli)
1 medium-size onion, peeled and chopped roughly
2–3 fresh green chillies, deseeded
dash of fresh lime juice
dash of water
sugar (optional)

1. Strip the mint leaves and very soft stems. Put into a blender or food processor.
2. Add the mooli roughly chopped. Reserve a small piece 1 cm (½ inch) long.
3. Add the onion and as many chillies as you wish. De–seed the chillies first. I find two chillies enough for me.
4. Blend or process to a purée. Stir in the reserved mooli, cut in wafer thin circles.
5. Add sugar to taste.

FRESH CARROT & COCONUT RELISH

5 ml (1 tsp) white mustard seeds
30 ml (2 tbsp) oil
½ fresh green chilli, de-seeded and chopped very finely
    (add more if you wish)
1.25 ml (¼ tsp) mustard powder
115 g (4 oz) freshly grated coconut
50 ml (2 fl oz) fresh lemon juice
2.5 ml (½ tsp) salt
450 g (1 lb) fresh, hard carrots, grated

1. Heat the oil in a frying pan and toss in the mustard seeds for a few seconds.
2. Add the coconut and chilli. Cook until the mixture is just beginning to colour.
3. Stir in the lemon juice, salt and carrots.
4. Chill and store in the fridge.

    Note: I find that grating a chunk of hard, fresh coconut is much easier with a round grater. I did try it in the food processor but it was just a bit too chunky – I then toasted the coconut and put it on a cake!

CHUTNEYS & PICKLES

Our national taste for chutney is one of the legacies of our days of Indian imperialism. My mother and father worked in India for many years and the first chutney I ever remember is the green and gold squared-off tall jar of mango chutney, still being sold. I do not know if the label still has a picture of a bewhiskered Indian soldier in an elaborate uniform and turban, and a little boy servant handing him the jar. The chutney was very sweet, a pale gold colour, with large pieces of 'hairy' mango. I know now that the hairs are just fibres but then I absolutely could not eat them for fear of eating something sinister. But I did like the sauce. Home-made mango chutney has a sharper, fresh flavour, and even the one made with canned fruit is not bad at all.

I cannot understand the national passion for the commercial chutney called a pickle which has no taste of any particular ingredient but a powerfully flavoured sauce made very dark indeed. One of the main ingredients of this pickle is turnip, a word that is not on the ingredients list except in its Latin form *rutabarga*. I don't know why this irritates me so much but it does, especially when I see giant jars of it sitting in every sandwich bar in the land. Chutneys and pickles are one of the easiest forms of cookery. It is difficult to make a mistake, except for the one to do with a wooden spoon. You simply must keep stirring – burnt chutney is pretty disgusting.

LEMON CHUTNEY
Yield 675 g (1¹/₂ lb)

3 large thin-skinned lemons, scrubbed
1 medium Spanish onion, peeled and finely chopped
1 Granny Smith eating apple, cored and chopped into small dice
175 g (6 oz) granulated sugar
115 g (4 oz) light coloured sultanas
2.5 cm (1 inch) square fresh ginger, peeled and finely diced
225–300 ml (8–10 fl oz) white wine vinegar

1. Use a sharp knife to pare off the lemon skins, and cut these into fine strips. Lemon peel is tough, so cover the peel with water and boil for a few minutes. Drain off the water and do this again. Drain and reserve the peel.
2. Over a bowl, as if you were peeling an apple, peel away and discard the white pith round each lemon. Chop the fruit up and pick out every seed you can find.
3. Put everything – zest, flesh, onion, apple, sugar, sultanas, ginger and most of the white wine vinegar – in a pan. Simmer for about 30–40 minutes, or until the raw onion is soft. You may not need all of the vinegar. Cook until there is almost no free liquid round the fruit.
4. Put into warm jars and cover with vinegar-proof lids.
5. Set aside for 3–4 weeks.

ORANGE CHUTNEY FOR CHEESE *Yield 1.3 kg (3 lb)*

This strongly-flavoured chutney is a perfect partner for a good English Cheddar cheese or cold duck. Use only thin-skinned oranges, which have much less pith than others. Use a zester to remove the peel, or use a razor-sharp knife to pare away the peel.

675 g (1$\frac{1}{2}$ lb) thin skinned oranges
225 g (8 oz) sultanas (pale gold ones if possible)
350 g (12 oz) Bramley apples, cored, peeled and chopped
350 g (12 oz) onions, peeled and chopped
425 ml (15 fl oz) white wine vinegar
5 ml (1 level tsp) mixed ground spice
2.5 ml ($\frac{1}{2}$ level tsp) salt
2.5 ml ($\frac{1}{2}$ level tsp) ground ginger
generous grating of nutmeg
225 g (8 oz) dark soft brown sugar

1. Peel the oranges of zest, or use a zester. Then chop the zest fairly small.
2. Now peel the oranges again to remove as much pith as possible. Discard the pith, then chop the fruit quite small. Make sure you save the juice.
3. Put the orange zest, juice, chopped fruit, apples and onions in a large pan. Cook uncovered until the onions are soft.
4. Remove the lid, stir in the sultanas, vinegar, ginger, salt, spice, nutmeg and sugar. Stir until the sugar dissolves, then simmer for about an hour, or until there is no free liquid.
5. Put into warm clean jars and cover.
6. Set aside to cool, then label with name and date.

RATATOUILLE CHUTNEY

Yield 1.3 kg (3 lb)

This chutney is successful when the ingredients are only just cooked but still retain their shape. I like to chop the ingredients in different ways. The white radish (mooli) is not a traditional ingredient but its pale colour and texture is attractive.

600 ml (20 fl oz) white wine vinegar
350 g (12 oz) granulated sugar
5 ml (1 tsp) whole allspice berries
5 ml (1 tsp) coriander seeds
5 ml (1 tsp) salt
2.5 ml ($^{1}/_{2}$ tsp) white mustard seed
4 medium size cloves garlic, peeled and finely chopped
350 g (12 oz) aubergine, wiped, topped and tailed,
**   and cut into chunks about the size of a sugar cube**
350 g (12 oz) tomatoes, skinned, de-seeded and chopped into small dice
350 g (12 oz) red pepper, de-seeded and cut into long strips
350 g (12 oz) very firm small courgettes, wiped, topped and tailed,
**   and sliced into chunky rings**
350 g (12 oz) onion, peeled and chopped into rings
1 medium size mooli (white radish), peeled and sliced into fine rings

1. Use a preserving pan and dissolve the sugar in the white wine vinegar.
2. Crush the allspice berries and the coriander seeds in a pestle and mortar, and stir these into the sweetened vinegar along with everything else.
3. Bring to a boil, then reduce to a simmer, leaving the pan uncovered. Timings vary, so keep an eye on the texture of the vegetables. There should be little or no liquid visible when the chutney is ready. Pot in the usual way.

PINEAPPLE CHUTNEY

Yield 1.3 kg (3 lb)

1 large pineapple – about 1.6 kg (3$^{1}/_{2}$ lb)
115 g (4 oz) onion, peeled and finely chopped
300 ml (10 fl oz) cider vinegar
280 g (10 oz) soft brown sugar
knife tip of chilli powder
5 ml (1 tsp) white mustard seeds
1.25 ml ($^{1}/_{4}$ tsp) ground cloves
1 cm ($^{1}/_{2}$ inch) fresh ginger, peeled and grated
150 ml (5 fl oz) dry sherry

1. Chop the pineapple into small, neat pieces. I find the easiest way is to slice the pineapple into 1 cm ($^1/2$ inch) slices with a long knife. Now use scissors over a bowl to catch the juice, and cut off the skin, then cut the flesh and discard the hard central core.
2. Stir all the ingredients into a roomy pan, except the sherry. Stir over a medium heat until the sugar has melted. Bring to a boil, then reduce the heat to a simmer until the mixture is thick. Remove from the heat.
3. Stir in the sherry and set aside to cool slightly.
4. Spoon into warm jars and cover in the usual way.

PICKLED GARLIC

Pickles are served throughout Asia as a counter-balance to the rich flavours and fiery heat of curry. In Korea, Thailand and India, pickled garlic is a firm favourite. The small, mild Chinese bulbs are pickled whole in rice vinegar, to be snapped apart as needed, eaten as a relish or cooked in stir-fries and stewed dishes.

Rice vinegar, like rice wine, is made from fermented glutinous rice. It has a mellow, slightly sweet flavour, but varies greatly in subtlety and colour. The closest western equivalent is cider vinegar – in which case we need extra sugar.

In this recipe, adapted from one from Ann and Franco Taruschio, of the celebrated Walnut Tree Inn, Monmouthshire, the garlic is lightly cooked and the vinegar sweetened. This produces mild, nutty cloves devoid of searing heat. It is a good way of preserving the new season's garlic.

80 cloves, peeled
150 ml (5 fl oz) cider vinegar
600 ml (1 pint) water
40 g ($1^1/2$ oz) granulated sugar
5 ml (1 level tsp) salt
1 small dried red chilli, or 1.25 ml ($^1/4$ tsp) dried chilli flakes

1. Bring the vinegar, water, sugar and salt to a boil, reduce the heat and add the chilli pepper. Simmer for 5 minutes.
2. Add garlic and boil for 1 minute.
3. Leave to cool and put into sterilised jars with some of the liquid.
4. Store for at least one week before eating. Store an opened jar in the fridge.

SWEET PICKLING VINEGAR

Spiced pickling vinegars are not often made at home now, since flavoured and spiced vinegars of all descriptions are readily available. I think we also tend to make pickles in smaller quantities with milder wine vinegars. However, this recipe is one which I find useful for:

Fresh apricots
Cut each fruit in two and remove the stone.

Fresh damsons
I tend to leave these whole but fish out any loose ones during the cooking. Mention on the label that there are some stones inside.

Onions
Small onions, or silverskins, peeled. It is easier to peel tiny onions if you pour boiling water over them first and allow them to cool, and then top and tail and remove the skins. This long, tedious job is for the very patient but you can also buy frozen peeled button onions too.

Oranges
Scrub the skins with hot water and slice very thinly. I'm sorry to say that I discard the two end pieces! But do discard the seeds as well.

Peaches
I peel, halve and quarter these and remove the stones.

Ingredients

1.2 litres (2 pints) white wine vinegar, or distilled white vinegar
750 g (1 lb 10 oz) white caster sugar
25 g (1 oz) whole cloves
25 g (1 oz) whole allspice berries
1 small piece dried root ginger, washed to remove the powdery outside,
    then bruised with something heavy to split the skin
5 cm (2 ins) cinnamon stick
4 small pieces of mace blades
piece of muslin in which to tie the spices

1. Set a large, heatproof bowl over a pan of cold water. Put in all the ingredients plus the spice bundle, and cover with a plate. Bring to a boil and stir the sugar to encourage it to dissolve.
2. Remove the pan from the heat and set it aside to cool for at least 3 hours.
3. Strain and bottle.

To use the above recipe, the method is the same for apricots, damsons, oranges, peaches and onions.

1. Put the vinegar in a saucepan, add the fruit and simmer until tender but not mushy.
2. Lift the fruit out with a perforated spoon and pack it into hot, clean jars. Do not fill to the top of the jar.
3. Boil the remaining vinegar rapidly in an uncovered pan until it is reduced by about one-third of its depth.
4. Fill the jars with the syrupy mixture. Push the fruit under the liquid, then seal with vinegar-proof lids.
5. Set aside for at least 6 weeks.

PIED PIPER'S PEPPERS

This colourful recipe will spice up any dish.

6 medium red peppers
6 medium yellow peppers
850 ml (1¹/₂ pint) white wine vinegar
15 ml (1 tbsp) black peppercorns
small bunch fresh parsley & thyme
2 bay leaves

1. Wipe each pepper and cut into two cups. Remove the seeds and the white membrane. Set the cups skin side up on a baking sheet under a hot grill.
2. When the cups are slightly blistered and blackish in places, take the tray out and allow to cool a bit.
3. Remove the skins, then pack tightly into warm jars.
4. Put the vinegar peppercorns and herbs in a pan and bring to a boil. Simmer for just 5 minutes.
5. Strain out the herbs and pour the hot, spiced vinegar over the peppers to cover.
6. Allow to go cold and then cover.

SWEET PICKLED CHERRIES

Leave the stalks on the cherries – they are then easier to eat. Mature for one month and eat up within 3 months. The cherries do tend to shrink after that time, and do not look quite so attractive. The taste is not affected.

1.1 kg (2$^{1}/_{2}$ lb) fresh dark cherries, with stalks on if possible
   (ripe but not soft)
1 cm ($^{1}/_{2}$ inch) piece of peeled, fresh ginger, sliced
300 ml (10 fl oz) mixed red and white wine vinegar
350 g (12 oz) unrefined light brown sugar
150 ml (5 fl oz) water

1. Put the ginger, wine vinegars, the sugar and the water in a pan and bring slowly to a boil. Stir to help the sugar to melt, now stir on a low heat uncovered.
2. Prepare the cherries by wiping each one with a damp paper towel, and cut each stalk down to about 2.5 cm (1 inch). Puncture the skins just once with a sharp needle. Pack the cherries tightly into small jars.
3. Continue to simmer the wine vinegar and sugar mixture so that it reduces slightly until thicker.
4. Allow to cool, then pour over the cherries and set the jars aside to go cold.
5. Cover with vinegar-proof lids and store. (See note above, in the introduction.)
6. Delicious with cold ham and pheasant.

PICKLED BANANAS

I had never thought of using bananas this way until I saw a recipe from which I made this version.

300 ml (10 fl oz) white wine vinegar
350 g (12 oz) soft brown sugar
knife end of turmeric powder
6 large cloves
2.5 ml ($^{1}/_{2}$ level tsp) freshly milled black pepper
2.5 ml ($^{1}/_{2}$ level tsp) ground nutmeg
4 cardamom pods
grated rind from one small lemon
1.8 kg (4 lb) firm bananas (about 12 bananas)

1. First make the sweet, spiced vinegar. Put the vinegar, sugar, turmeric, cloves, black pepper, nutmeg and lemon rind in a roomy pan over a medium heat.
2. Bruise the four cardamom pods in your mortar and drop them in as well. Stir until the sugar dissolves. You may wish to add a little more turmeric if the first bit wasn't enough.
3. Bring to a boil for 4–5 minutes, then simmer for another 5 minutes.
4. Peel and slice the bananas chunkily and at an angle. Pack into warm jars.
5. Strain the hot vinegar into a hot jug and pour over the bananas to cover.
6. Allow to go cold before putting on lids.

BALSAMIC PICKLED ONIONS

Balsamic vinegar is an expensive, long-matured vinegar with a delicious mild flavour. It is a speciality of Modena, in Italy, but is now produced in many other countries including Britain.

900 g (2 lb) pickling or button onions
    (you can sometimes get frozen and peeled small onions)
425 ml (15 fl oz) cold water
150 ml (5 fl oz) balsamic vinegar
600 ml (20 fl oz) distilled white vinegar
55 g (2 oz) granulated sugar
55 g (2 oz) salt

1. Soak the onions in hot water for about 10 minutes. This makes them easier to peel. Drain and peel.
2. Stir the salt into 300 ml (10 fl oz) of the cold water.
3. Now take the other 150 ml (5 fl oz) water and warm it in a small pan. Dissolve the sugar in this.
4. Then stir the mixture back into the 300 ml (10 fl oz) of cold salty water.
5. Add the 600 ml (20 fl oz) distilled white vinegar and the balsamic vinegar. Set this liquid aside.
6. Using fresh water, barely cover the onions and poach them gently for about 10 minutes. Remove the onions when they are just beginning to soften.
7. Now spoon the onions into jars and pour the sweetened vinegar over the top.
8. Cover with vinegar-proof lids.

Maturing: This is a matter of choice – from 3 weeks to 3 months. Onions get very soft eventually and lose their appeal for me. I prefer them very slightly crunchy.

SLIPPY JIMS

Yield 1.1 kg (2½ lb)

If you ever have a glut of cucumbers, this way of preserving them will appeal to you. I got the recipe from food writer Rosemary Stark, who in turn brought it from America – hence the lovely name. My version is slightly different again.

2 very large, firm cucumbers
25 g (1 oz) cooking salt
225 g (8 fl oz) white wine vinegar and unsweetened raspberry vinegar, mixed
85 g (3 oz) white granulated sugar
10 ml (2 tsp) light mustard seeds
5 ml (1 tsp) celery seeds
1 small dried red chilli pepper

1. Top and tail the cucumbers and wipe them with damp kitchen paper. Cut each in two lengthways. Using a sharp teaspoon, scoop out the seeds and discard them.
2. Cut each half cucumber into either 2 or 3 chunks, depending on the height of your glass jars. The pickled cucumber sticks look best standing up straight in the jars. Now cut each chunk into 4 strips.
3. Scatter the cooking salt over the cucumbers in a flat dish. Turn them over and over with your hands, so that the salt reaches every surface. Set the dish aside for at least 2 hours.
4. Meanwhile, make the spiced vinegar. Put the sugar, seeds and vinegars in a stainless steel or enamel-lined pan which is big enough to hold all the cucumber sticks later. Over a low heat, stir the vinegars and dissolve the sugar.
5. Now rinse the cucumber sticks and dry them. Slip the dried strips into the flavoured vinegar and simmer until the creamy flesh of the cucumbers becomes translucent.
6. When cool enough to handle, pack the sticks of cucumber into clean, warm jars.
7. Add a few mustard seeds from the pan for decoration and top up with spiced vinegar.
8. Slip a fragment of the dried chilli pepper skin carefully down the side of each jar.
9. Leave to go cold, then cover with vinegar-proof lids.

OTHER ACCOMPANIMENTS

This is a real mixed bag of all sorts of ideas which would not fit easily under the other headings.

I particularly commend to you the section on OLIVES (page 58). You can buy the spiced and flavoured versions but they are expensive. Try doing it yourself, especially if you are having a crowd in. Buy your olives loose or in a large jar. They keep for a long time but I can guarantee that your flavoured olives will disappear in no time at all.

POTATO CRISPS

I have often been asked about making your own potato crisps at home. In fact, we once had as a monthly competition – the biggest home-made crisp you can make. It is an interesting exercise.

The crisps have to be cut wafer thin. You would find it easier using a mandoline – a type of slicing gadget with a long blade. The crisps have to be dried very carefully. I found it easier to rinse them in cold water before drying them. They fry easily in oil but do not crowd the pan. They brown very quickly, so aim to get them out and on to kitchen paper to drain while still golden.

They do taste wonderful with a sprinkling of sea salt – you can tell they are made from a potato. I know at least 2 famous London hotels where they pride themselves on their crisps. The Dorchester is one and I think the Connaught is the other.

OLIVES

If you like olives and all the varieties of flavoured olives so common in Spain, you will enjoy trying out these for special occasions. The recipes are based on ones I first saw in a Spanish journal. You can buy black and green olives loose or in jars or tins. Add just enough oil to coat the olives and no more. Serve with a pre-dinner drink or as part of a cold buffet.

OLIVES & RED PEPPER

250 g (9 oz) green olives, stuffed with pimento (red pepper)
140 g (5 oz) fresh red pepper
small knob fresh ginger, peeled and grated
2.5 ml ($^1/_2$ tsp) paprika
1.25 ml ($^1/_4$ tsp) ground cumin
50 ml (2 fl oz) fresh lemon juice
splash of virgin olive oil

1. Drain the olives and put them in a serving dish.
2. Wipe and de-seed the pepper. Remove the white membrane from inside. Chop $^3/_4$ of the pepper into small dice, and the last $^1/_4$ into fine strips. Set the strips on one side.
3. Into another bowl, grate the ginger. Stir in the paprika, cumin, lemon juice and the oil. Stir these flavourings thoroughly, then stir them into the olives.
4. Set aside for an hour, then taste and adjust the flavourings.
5. Decorate with the reserved strips of pepper.

OLIVES & PARMA HAM   *Serves 6*

250 g (9 oz) green olives
85 g (3 oz) Parma ham
6 small pickled gherkins
15 ml (1 level tbsp) fresh dill, chopped
5 ml (1 level tsp) fresh parsley, chopped
dash of virgin olive oil

1. Drain the olives and cut them into rings.
2. Use scissors to chop the ham into very fine strips. Add these to the olives.
3. Slice the gherkins longways and add them with the chopped dill and parsley.
4. Stir well and add the virgin olive oil.

MINTED GREEN OLIVES

Serves 4–6

250 g (9 oz) green unstuffed olives
15 ml (1 tbsp) sesame seeds
1 medium size sweet orange
5 ml (1 tsp) black peppercorns
15 ml (1 heaped tbsp) fresh mint, chopped
dash of virgin olive oil

1. On a baking sheet, toast the sesame seeds either under a grill or in a hot oven. Watch them carefully, as they soon burn.
2. Drain the olives and put them into a bowl.
3. Sprinkle the sesame seeds over the olives.
4. Now pare about half the peel off the orange as finely as you can. If you use a zester, do not dig too deeply. Finely chop or slice the peel, and add this to the bowl.
5. Take a sharp knife and peel the orange as if you were peeling an apple, then slice the orange into rings.
6. Use scissors to chop out the bits of orange, discarding the seeds and the pith.
7. Add these orange bits to the olive bowl with the mint.
8. Crush the peppercorns in a pestle and mortar. Stir them in with a dash of oil. Stir well.

SPICY BLACK OLIVES

Serves 4–6

250 g (9 oz) stoned black olives
2 sticks crisp celery, washed and finely chopped
$^1/_2$ small onion, finely sliced
2 small bay leaves
5 ml (1 tsp) fresh thyme leaves
50 ml (2 fl oz) sweet white wine
50 ml (2 fl oz) sherry vinegar (or white wine vinegar)
5 ml (1 tsp) black peppercorns
dash of virgin olive oil

1. Drain the olives and put them in a serving bowl with the celery, onion, bay leaves, thyme leaves, sweet wine and sherry vinegar.
2. Crush the peppercorns in a pestle and mortar, and add to the bowl.
3. Lastly add a dash of virgin olive oil. Stir well.

PICKLED SUGAR

Yield 900 g (2 lb)

This unusual recipe uses a type of seaweed sometimes called sugar wrack. The Latin name is *Laminaria Saccharina*. I assume the origin must be Chinese. There is no sugar in the ingredients list. The sweetness comes from the seaweed itself, as the Latin name suggests. To make it, you would need an illustrated guide to seaweeds. I tasted it in a small pub in Devon. Pick a frond while it is light in colour and not too leathery.

1 sugar wrack frond
1 medium onion, peeled and sliced thinly
1 small mooli (Chinese white radish) about 450 g (1 lb), peeled and thinly sliced
1 cm ($^1/_2$ inch) fresh ginger, peeled and diced
1.25 ml ($^1/_4$ tsp) turmeric
300 ml (10 fl oz) rice vinegar (or cider vinegar)
15 ml (1 tbsp) oil

1. Bring the oil and cider vinegar to a boil and whisk in the turmeric. Set aside to go cold.
2. Wash the seaweed carefully in plenty of fresh water, then fold it tightly in a roll and slice as thinly as possible.
3. Heat about 1 cm ($^1/_2$ inch) oil in a large frying pan and sauté the white radish slices and the onion until they soften slightly. Do not fully cook.
4. Lastly, toss in the sliced seaweed for just a minute or so.
5. Drain off the oil, sprinkle the diced ginger into the mixture.
6. Pack tightly into jars.
7. Pour the cooled vinegar over to cover.
8. Set aside for at least 2 weeks. Use as a pickle.

PICKLED ONION RINGS

Serves 6–8

This recipe was given to me by an Indian lady food writer who cooked with me on TV. I've used it often, and it will liven up any rice dish. The harshness of raw onions disappears.

225 g (8 oz) Spanish onion, peeled and separated into rings
$^1/_2$ fresh green chilli, de-seeded and finely chopped
50 ml (2 fl oz) fresh lemon juice
2.5 ml ($^1/_2$ tsp) salt
freshly ground pepper

1. Mix all the ingredients together and set aside for 2 hours to allow the onion rings to go limp and the flavour to have developed.
2. This will keep for about 5 days.

PICKLED VEGETABLES

Yield 900 g (2 lb)

Though not strictly a preserve, this mixture will keep for a week in the fridge. Cut the mooli into thin rounds, then use a tiny fluted cutter on the slices. Cut the other vegetables in different ways, such as batons or cubes. These look very pretty served with other appetizers on a flat dish with things like hot mini spring rolls or spiced prawns. This sort of pickle is very common in Chinese cooking.

1 small courgette
1 carrot
1 mooli (Chinese white radish)
1 lotus root (or substitute quartered radishes)
300 ml (10 fl z) rice vinegar (or white wine vinegar)
sugar to taste

1. Prepare all the vegetables carefully and pack into a large jar or jug.
2. Bring the vinegar to a boil. Remove from the heat and stir in sugar according to your taste.
3. Allow the sweetened vinegar to go cold before you pour it over the vegetables.
4. You can add a little water to the sweetened vinegar if you find it too strong.

CHINESE DIPPING SAUCE

A favourite Chinese dish is boiled or poached chicken, and this sauce would be ideal to eat with it.

75 ml (5 tbsp) light Soy sauce
20 ml (4 tsp) oyster sauce
10 ml (2 tsp) finely chopped fresh ginger
10 ml (2 tsp) finely chopped fresh garlic
10 ml (2 tsp) finely chopped spring onion

1. Mix well.
2. Taste and adjust the flavouring.

HOT DOG MUSTARD

Yield 300 ml (10 fl oz)

You can vary the flavour of this mustard by adding Worcester sauce, or chilli sauce. It is safer to cook it in a double boiler or in a heat-proof bowl over a pan of simmering water.

45 ml (3 tbsp) powdered mustard
30 ml (2 tbsp) demerara sugar
15 ml (1 tbsp) plain flour
1 large egg, beaten
250 ml (9 fl oz) white vinegar (or flavoured vinegar, if you wish)

1. In the upper pan of a double boiler (or in a heat-proof basin), mix together the mustard, sugar and flour, followed by the beaten egg and the vinegar. Stir thoroughly and often, and cook until the mixture thickens.
2. Allow to cool, and put in small jars.
3. Store in a fridge.

CRUNCHY PEANUT & HORSERADISH DIP

30 ml (2 level tbsp) crunchy peanut butter
5 ml (1 level tsp) creamed horseradish
60 ml (4 tbsp) natural yoghurt
30 ml (2 tbsp) good mayonnaise

Spoon all the ingredients into a bowl and stir together.

MUSTARD & DILL DIP

15 ml (1 level tbsp) grain mustard (from a jar)
1 clove garlic, crushed, or 1 tsp ready prepared garlic (from a jar)
150 ml (5 fl oz) fromage frais
15 ml (1 level tbsp) chopped fresh dill fronds
knife tip of chilli sauce
touch of sugar, if you wish

Beat all the ingredients together and set aside for about an hour, for the flavours to mellow.

HERB SALTS

Herbed salts are used to add extra flavour to a salad. Make up in small quantities and use fairly quickly.

1. Just add the chopped fresh but dry herb to sea salt or ordinary table salt.
2. Pour into a jar with a lid, and shake it daily for a week.
3. Then pour the salt onto a baking sheet covered with non-stick baking paper, and dry it in a very low oven.

Sage, basil and thyme leaves are all suitable, so are finely chopped rosemary needles.

Basil, Thyme: 5 ml (1 level tsp) chopped herb to 30 ml (2 big tbsp) salt

Sage, Rosemary: 2.5 ml ($\frac{1}{2}$ level tsp) is plenty for 30 ml (2 big tbsp) salt

SPICED NUTS

I made these last Christmas – they were eaten up in no time at all. It is infinitely cheaper than buying them, too. Use brown-skinned almonds. Skin them yourself by dropping them into boiling water. Leave until you can handle them, when the skin should slip off easily. If you use ready-skinned nuts, try to soak them in the water for several hours to soften them. Use a measure for the spices.

10 ml (2 tsp) vegetable oil
2.5 ml ($\frac{1}{2}$ tsp) ground coriander
2.5 ml ($\frac{1}{2}$ tsp) ground cumin
1.25 ml ($\frac{1}{4}$ tsp) ground cayenne pepper
1.25 ml ($\frac{1}{4}$ tsp) ground turmeric
115 g (4 oz) brown-skinned almonds
115 g (4 oz) plain cashew nuts
115 g (4 oz) pecan nuts
salt

1. Heat a heavy-based frying pan over a medium heat. Add the oil, then stir in the four ground spices.
2. Cook for just 1 minute, then toss in the nuts. Fry, turning the nuts over and over until lightly brown.
3. Sprinkle salt over the nuts very lightly. Set them to dry out on non-stick paper.
4. Store in a sealed jar.

LEMONS PRESERVED IN OLIVE OIL

Scrubbed lemons freeze very well but try a pot of these. I find the small, thin-skinned lemons sold in nets are best. Sliced very finely and chopped, the flavoured lemons make a delicious addition to a salad dressing. You do not need much – about $\frac{1}{2}$ a teaspoon per person to give a lovely note. Try mixing into sweet salad dressings prior to tossing the salad leaves. The lemon-flavoured oil will also be a delicious base for salad dressings and mayonnaise.

5 fresh lemons
8 cloves
olive oil

1. Scrub and dry the lemons and cut one into two halves.
2. Stick about 4 cloves in each lemon and push them all into a big jar.
3. Push the lemons down tightly, then cover with the oil.
4. Set aside for about 4 weeks.
5. Store in the fridge after opening.

PRESERVED LEMON WEDGES

Look for small thin-skinned, roundish lemons, rather than the big ones with pointed ends. The ones sold in nets are usually of the small kind.

12 small lemons
55 g (2 oz) Maldon salt (or sea salt)
5 cloves
10 coriander seeds
10 peppercorns
3 bay leaves (not fresh)
7.5 cm (3 ins) cinnamon stick, broken in two

1. Cut 6 of the lemons into quarters and rub the cut edges with a little of the salt.
2. Now pack the lemons tightly into a big jar (1.2 litre / 2 pint preserving jar).
3. Drop in all the salt and spices. Squeeze the juice from the other 6 lemons. Push the lemons down under the surface. Add the rest of the juice.
4. Set the jar aside and cover for 2 weeks. Give the jar a shake or a stir every other day to dissolve the salt.
5. Before using, rinse the lemons in water and pat dry on kitchen paper.
6. Store in a fridge or cold larder.

SAGE & APPLE SAUCE

Sage grows easily in the garden. Try to use the fresh leaves rather than the dried herb. Wonderful with pork or pork sausage.

2 medium size cooking apples (Bramley type)
4 large sage leaves
sugar and salt

1. Peel and core the apples and simmer them in a little water until they 'fall'.
2. Beat into a smoothish purée.
3. Stir in the sage leaves and add a small amount of sugar and salt to taste.
4. Cool and serve.
5. Will store in a jar in the fridge for 2 days.

ROSEMARY & TOMATO SAUCE

Rosemary grows easily and has pretty blue flowers in the summer. It is a powerful herb, so use it with discretion.

1 medium onion, peeled and finely chopped
1 small clove garlic, peeled and crushed
oil
500 g (1 lb 2 oz) ripe tomatoes
3–4 sprigs of rosemary – small ones

1. In a pan, fry the onion and garlic in a little oil until soft.
2. Peel the tomatoes by dropping them first into boiling water and then into cold. The skins should slip off easily. De-seed and discard the seeds. Chop the flesh into small pieces, discarding any green stalk.
3. Add the onion and garlic mixture along with the rosemary. Then add just a dash of water if the mixture is dry. Simmer for about 10 minutes, stirring often.
4. Season with salt and freshly ground pepper.
5. Fish out the rosemary.
6. Serve hot or cold as an accompaniment to fish, fish cakes or with freshly cooked pasta.
7. Will store for up to one week in the fridge.

NO-COOK BARBECUE SAUCE (1)

While not actually a preserve, this mixture makes a good marinade for pork chops, spare ribs or lamb chops. Use as a basting sauce, as the meat cooks, and as a pouring sauce to serve with the finished dish.

45 ml (3 tbsp) Soy sauce
250 ml (9 fl oz) pineapple juice
2.5 ml ($^1/_2$ tsp) garlic salt
1.25 ml ($^1/_4$ tsp) white pepper
15 ml (1 tbsp) brown sugar

1. Stir together all the ingredients and mix thoroughly.
2. Store in the fridge and use within 2 days.

NO-COOK BARBECUE SAUCE (2)   *Yield 1.2 litres (2 pints)*

200 ml (7 fl oz) Tomato Ketchup
90 ml (3 fl oz) chilli sauce, or to taste
75 ml (5 tbsp) English mustard powder
225 ml (8 fl oz) white wine vinegar
150 ml (5 fl oz) lemon juice
75 ml (5 tbsp) bottled brown sauce
$^1/_2$ can export beer
10 ml (2 tsp) Soy sauce
15 ml (1 tbsp) vegetable oil
dash of tabasco sauce
30 ml (2 tbsp) Worcester sauce

1. Stir together all the ingredients and mix thoroughly.
2. Store in fridge or freezer in small quantities. Use within 2–3 weeks.

CARAMEL SAUCE

This sauce would be lovely with individual steamed chocolate puddings or poured over ice cream or sweet pancakes. Use a deep pan, as the caramel starts to spit when you add the cream.

225 g (8 oz) caster sugar
45 ml (3 tbsp) water
300 ml (¹/₂ pint) double cream

1. In a heavy pan, melt the sugar in the water. Simmer until the colour of the sugary water turns deep gold. The darker it is, the stronger the flavour, but take care – it does burn easily.
2. Remove the pan from the heat. Stir the cream in the carton so that it is liquid and slowly whisk it into the caramel. I use a small loop-headed whisk.
3. Set aside to go cold.
4. Will keep for 2 days in a jar in the fridge.

RICH CARAMEL SAUCE WITH WALNUTS

This cooked sauce is good as a dip for fresh strawberries (leave the green top on to make them easier to hold). It is also nice over plain ice cream.

85 g (3 oz) soft brown sugar
small can evaporated milk – 175 ml (6 oz)
15 ml (1 tbsp) cornflour
60 ml (4 tbsp) water
40 g (1¹/₂ oz) butter
40 g (1¹/₂ oz) finely chopped pale walnuts

1. Put the sugar and evaporated milk in a heavy pan. Check that the sugar is lump free. Heat gently and stir to melt the sugar.
2. In a small bowl, mix the 60 ml (4 tbsp) cornflour with the water until it is smooth. Stir this into the sugar and milk and keep stirring until it thickens.
3. Add the butter and nuts and set aside until needed.
4. Will store in the fridge for 2 days. Stir well before you use it and serve warm rather than cold.

LEMON & BALSAMIC VINEGAR DRESSING

If you have ever seen the TV chefs dribbling a dark dressing round their creations, it is often something like this. Citrus oils are stunningly flavoursome. You can buy them in little bottles in lemon, lime and orange. Balsamic vinegar is a long-matured vinegar of high quality.

15 ml (1 tbsp) lemon oil
15 ml (1 tbsp) balsamic vinegar

Whisk together and use sparingly.

RAITA

These sauces, usually served with Indian food, are based on natural yoghurt.

CUCUMBER RAITA

350 ml (12 fl oz) plain yoghurt
1 medium cucumber
15 ml (1 large tbsp) chopped fresh mint leaves
salt & pepper
sugar

1. Put the yoghurt into a bowl.
2. Peel the cucumber and sprinkle with salt.
3. Grate the cucumber into a small bowl. Drain off the excess liquid. Add the drained cucumber and mint to the yoghurt.
4. Season with salt and pepper to taste.
5. Add a couple of pinches of sugar and taste again.
6. Stir well and set aside until the flavours meld together.
7. Serve cool and store for just 2 days. Mix well before serving.

VARIATIONS (instead of cucumber):

    a) Grated carrot
    b) Coriander leaves, finely chopped
    c) Spring onions, chopped
    d) Green mango (under-ripe mango), chopped
    e) Tomato, diced, peeled, de-seeded and chopped

BLUE CHEESE DRESSING
FOR GRILLED OR BARBECUED STEAK

85 g (3 oz) soft blue cheese (dolcelatte is my favourite)
15 ml (1 tbsp) white wine vinegar
45 ml (3 tbsp) walnut oil (or olive oil)
60 ml (4 tbsp) double cream
30 ml (2 tbsp) finely chopped parsley
black pepper

1. Beat up the cheese and add all the ingredients. A stick blender makes a smooth job of it.
2. Add more cream if you want a milder taste.
3. Best eaten within 2 days. Beat again before serving.

BASIL LEAF SAUCE FOR SALMON

You need a lot of fresh basil leaves for this sauce. It tastes just wonderful and the brilliant green looks terrific with the pretty pink of a poached salmon steak or fillet. A food processor or a stick blender makes this sauce child's play.

40 g (1½ oz) fresh basil leaves
60–90 ml (4–6 tbsp) olive oil
15 ml (1 tbsp) lemon juice (or white wine vinegar)
salt and black pepper

1. Rinse the basil leaves in cold water and pat dry in a tea towel. Put them into the food processor and reduce to a purée.
2. Add the lemon juice and oil gradually, beating well.
3. Season to taste and use on the day it is made.

PEANUT SAUCE

This easily made sauce is perfect for kebabs. It is also nice as a dip for tortilla chips or pieces of garlic bread.

250 ml (9 fl oz) water
15 ml (1 tbsp) dark brown sugar
250 g (9 oz) peanut butter (either smooth or chunky)
1 fresh lime – juice and zest
15 ml (1 tbsp) soy sauce

1. Dissolve the sugar in the water with the lime zest. Warm gently to help this..
2. Remove from the heat and beat in all the other ingredients. Use a food processor or a stick blender if you have one.
3. This sauce will keep in the fridge for 4–5 days.
4. Beat well before you serve.

GRAND MARNIER & MASCARPONE SAUCE

This uncooked cream sauce would be delicious over fresh or lightly stewed fruit like nectarines, peaches or apricots. Another orange liqueur, like Cointreau, would be good too.

225 g (8 oz) Mascarpone (Italian soft cream cheese)
125 ml (4 fl oz) double cream
7.5 ml (1$^{1}/_{2}$ tspn) caster sugar
2 drops of good quality vanilla extract
dash of Grand Marnier

1. Beat all the ingredients together.
2. Taste and adjust the sweetness to suit you.
3. Store in a jar in the fridge for 2–3 days.

SPICED GREEN PEPPERCORN SAUCE

This lovely savoury sauce was devised by a fellow food writer on the *Yorkshire Post*, called Stephen Jackson. He served it with chargrilled venison steaks. Green peppercorns are under-ripe peppercorns which are soft, and you can buy them preserved in small jars.

100 ml (3¹/₂ fl oz) Port
30 ml (2 tbsp) green peppercorns, dried
30 ml (2 tbsp) raisins
15 ml (1 tbsp) dark molasses sugar
2.5 ml (¹/₂ tsp) ground cinnamon
2.5 ml (¹/₂ tsp) ground nutmeg
salt & pepper

1. Simmer all the ingredients very gently and serve warm.
2. Store in a jar for 4–5 days if necessary.

BALSAMIC DRESSING FOR COS LETTUCE LEAVES

This dressing is strongly flavoured to cope with the sturdy cos lettuce leaves. Dribble the dressing very lightly.

60 ml (4 tbsp) best quality olive oil
5 ml (1 level tsp) sugar
22.5 ml (1¹/₂ tbsp) balsamic vinegar
salt & pepper
15 ml (1 tbsp) chopped fresh herbs

Mix all the above ingredients together. Whisk well before serving.

SWEET AND SOUR DRESSING SAUCE
FOR CHINESE CRISPY PANCAKES
OR INDIAN SAMOSAS

3 spring onions, topped and tailed and very finely sliced
1 very small clove garlic, peeled and crushed
1 very small green chilli, de-seeded and finely chopped
5 ml (1 level tsp) caster sugar
15 ml (1 tbsp) soy sauce
finely grated zest and juice of 2 lemons
5 ml (1 tsp) tomato pulp

1. Put all the ingredients in a pan. Bring to a boil, then simmer for just a minute, then turn off the heat.
2. Serve cool rather than hot.

CLOTTED CREAM

You can make your own clotted cream very easily.

600 ml (1 pint) Jersey milk (sometimes called 'Breakfast Milk')

1. Pour the milk into a heavy based pan. Cover the pan and leave in a cool place for 12 hours in summer and 24 hours in winter.
2. Gently lift the pan to the cooker. Heat very gently for 45 minutes but do not boil.
3. When a solid ring of clotted cream forms round the edge of the pan and the surface is all wrinkled, it is ready.
4. Leave to cool for another 24 hours.
5. Skim the cream from the pan with a slotted spoon and serve.

   Note: The whey left behind makes excellent scones or bread.

GARLIC & MAYONNAISE DRESSING

Mayonnaise can be the base for many differently flavoured dressings. This one with garlic would be good with crisply fried goujons (strips) of sole or haddock.

90 ml (6 tbsp) mayonnaise
15 ml (1 tbsp) natural yoghurt
1 large or 2 small cloves garlic, peeled and finely chopped
15 ml (1 tbsp) freshly chopped parsley
salt & pepper

1. Stir all the ingredients together.
2. Allow to stand for 3–4 hours to allow the garlic flavour to percolate.

VARIATIONS (instead of garlic):

   a) Chopped cucumber and a pinch of chilli powder.
   b) Extra parsley or other herbs like chives.
   c) A large tablespoon of well-fried onions.
   d) Grated carrot.

ONION MARMALADE

This, of course, is not really a marmalade, but is a delicious accompaniment to most grilled dishes.

900 g (2 lb) Spanish onions, peeled and sliced
150 ml (5 fl oz) red wine
30 ml (2 tbsp) red wine vinegar
15 ml (1 tbsp) grain mustard
2 cloves garlic, peeled and finely chopped
15 ml (1 tbsp) soft brown sugar

1. Put all the ingredients in a pan and cook gently until the onion is extremely soft. Stir often.
2. Taste and adjust the seasoning, adding more sugar if you wish.
3. Store in a covered jar in the fridge and eat within a week.

PARSLEY HONEY
Yield 425 ml ($^3/_4$ pint)

Parsley is rich in iron and this is an old recipe used as a tonic. It does not actually jell like a jelly but is more like runny honey. This is something to try when you have an abundance of healthy, bright parsley.

140 g (5 oz) fresh parsley, stalks and all
850 ml (1$^1/_2$ pints) water
900 g (2 lb) granulated sugar
5 ml (1 small tsp) white wine vinegar

1. Rinse the parsley under a cold running tap and shake dry in a tea towel.
2. Measure out just 600 ml (1 pint) water and, using the handle of a wooden spoon, stand it in the water, then mark the water line with a pencil.
3. Add another 300 ml ($^1/_2$ pint) water to the pan and push in all the parsley. Chop the stalks to get them into the pan. Bring to a boil, then reduce to a lively simmer, uncovered, until the liquid has reduced to 600 ml (1 pint). Use your wooden spoon measurement to check.
4. Strain through a nylon sieve and rinse out the pan. Bring the juice to a boil and stir in the sugar. When it has all dissolved, reduce to a simmer until the mixture goes syrupy.
5. Stir in the vinegar. Pot and cover.

FRUIT AND SPIRITS

SLOE GIN

Sloe gin is a charming pink colour and is particularly appreciated at Christmas, served in tiny, pretty glasses. You can use an old, tall Kilner jar – the 1.8 kg (4 lb) size would be fine.

225 g (8 oz) fresh sloe berries (unwrinkled)
700 ml (1 bottle) cheap gin
115 g (4 oz) caster sugar
2–3 drops real almond essence

1. The berries have to be rinsed, patted dry and pricked with a needle. (To avoid this dreary chore, you can put the berries in the freezer overnight. Next day, when they defrost, you will find the skins have split.)
2. Put the berries in the jar with the almond essence, and pour over the gin. Cover the jar and set it aside for at least 2 months. Give it a good stir every now and then, and crush the berries with the spoon.
3. Strain the gin through two layers of muslin in a nylon sieve, or use a coffee filter paper.
4. When the gin is clear, stir in the sugar. Wait until it has dissolved before bottling. Taste the sloe gin – you may wish to add more sugar.

   Notes:
   a) You can also use vodka in this recipe, instead of gin, or damsons, instead of sloes.

   b) You can make strawberry or raspberry brandy in the same way as above, but less sugar will be needed. Start off with just 55 g (2 oz) and check the flavour. A small glass poured over vanilla ice cream would be delicious with a few fresh berries on the side.

ORANGE GIN

3 Seville oranges (available only in January or February)
2 fresh, thin-skinned lemons
1.2 litres (2 pints) gin
225 g (8 oz) sugar, or to taste

1. Wash and dry the fruit, then pare off the rinds as thinly as possible.
2. Put these into a large non-metal jug with the sugar and the gin. Stir this mixture every day for a couple of weeks, using a clean wooden spoon. Press the skins hard to release the flavour.
3. Taste the gin and add more sugar if you wish.
4. Strain carefully and bottle.
5. Delicious served neat and on the rocks. This is also excellent in a gin and tonic.

QUINCE CORDIAL

Cydonia Oblonga is said to be the best variety for its fruits. Pick in October and rinse off any surface 'fluff'.

Quinces
gin or vodka
caster sugar

1. Slice away any blemishes and chop the ripe quinces into a tall preserving jar.
2. Pour in either gin or vodka to barely cover.
3. Add 1 tbsp caster sugar for each quince.
4. Stir this mixture, cover and set it aside for at least one month.
   Shake every now and then to encourage the sugar to dissolve.
5. Strain through a nylon sieve and bottle.
6. Serve by pouring a good dash over ice cubes in the bottom of the glass.
   Top with fizzy water or soda and a slice of lime.

   Note: The fruits of the Japanese quince, or Japonica, which are various species of *Chaenomeles,* do not have much flavour.

GLOSSARY

BEEF TOMATO
These are the huge fat tomatoes which imitate the huge knobbly Italian ones which actually have twice the flavour.

BLUEBERRY
This round fat blackish berry is another import from America. I always find it lacking in much flavour but its looks are impressive and it adds colour to many mixed fruit salads and preserves.

BULGAR, OR CRACKED WHEAT
This fine grain is used a lot in Middle Eastern food. It does not need to be cooked, just soaked until it swells up. The texture is like very fine pasta. Very good for salads.

CAPERS
You can buy little pots of these highly flavoured green buds pickled. They come from a Mediterranean shrub, and were traditionally used for caper sauce for mutton. They are now used as a powerful flavouring. You can be a thrifty preserver by gathering the seed heads from nasturtiums. Pickle these in the usual way. They make an excellent substitute but it takes a long time to collect the buds in any number.

CHUTNEY
A chutney is a vinegar preserve which offers great scope for individuality by the maker. It is a mixture of fruits, fresh and dried, vegetables, sugar, vinegar and spices, cooked slowly together to form a thick jam-like consistency. A good chutney should have a mellow, mature flavour.

CONSERVE
This is usually not a true preserve, in that it is lower in sugar and does not have as firm a set as jam. However the soft set is ideal for many uses and the flavour should be intense. It must be stored in a fridge. Generally, the fruit is whole.

CORN CHIPS ·
Similar to our potato crisps but made with maize.

GLOSSARY

CRANBERRY
Sold fresh in early winter, this jewel-like red berry comes from America. We associate it strongly with cranberry sauce for our Christmas turkey. It is also excellent in preserves and its sharp flavour is a good contrast in many puddings. It freezes extremely well.

CRUDITEES
Raw vegetables cut into neat sticks or florets suitable for dips; eg. carrots, young turnip, cauliflower florets, sweet pepper sticks in yellow, red, green or orange, small mushrooms, celery.

CURDS
Contain eggs and butter in addition to the fruit and sugar, and are not intended to keep. Strictly speaking they are not a true preserve.

CRYSTALLISED GINGER
This is the same cooked and cooled knobs of sweet ginger as in stem ginger. It is rolled in sugar and allowed to dry. Both are popular and traditional Christmas gifts.

GELATINE, POWDERED
This comes loose in a small tin or in pre-packed sealed envelopes which contain enough to set 600 ml (1 pint) juice or pulp.

GUAVA
This greenish yellow fruit is from Brazil and has a wonderful perfume when ripe. It looks a bit like a small pear, and when cut in two there are a large number of seeds which have to be sieved out. Apart from use for preserves, the pulp could be used in ice-cream and puddings. It has a delicate flavour.

JALAPENO CHILLIES
One of the many varieties of very hot chilli peppers from South America. Use with care. It is a good idea to use rubber gloves when chopping or de-seeding any hot peppers, even the dried ones. You just have to rub the corner of your eye with a finger which has been in touch with a chilli to find you develop an instant painful irritation.

GLOSSARY

LIMES

Like lemons but smaller and bright green. The skins should be tight and the fruit juicy. Do not buy any wrinkled fruit. The flavour is sharp but not quite as acidic as lemons. The juice can be used in all the ways that lemon juice is used.

MANGO

Have you heard the old joke about eating a mango? – the only place to do this is in the bath! This is the finest of the exotic fruits we now import. The flesh is orange if very ripe; it is also squashy and juicy. There is a huge stone in a mango. Cut up the fruit by standing it on end and slicing down on each side of the stone to get at the fruit. The fruit clings tightly round the stone, so you need patience. Tinned mango is also quite good.

MOOLI

This used to be found only in Asian and Chinese supermarkets. It looks just like a white carrot or a refined parsnip. It is delicious peeled and grated in a salad or chopped into dice and added to a mixed vegetable dish.

MUSLIN OR NYLON

Used to tie up bundles of flavouring herbs or orange pips – for example, in marmalade. Two or three layers of muslin will be needed to make a good seal. I tend to use a very fine mesh nylon curtaining. Tie the bundles up 'Dick Whittington style', with fine string or, best of all, linen thread.

NECTARINE

Related to the peach family but with a smooth, silky skin. Like peaches, nectarines are sometimes rather woolly inside and, instead of a luscious fruit, you might have a poor thing with little flavour. Like apricots, you can sometimes rescue the fruit with some gentle stewing, very little sugar, and the merest hint of a drop of vanilla. In perfect condition and eaten raw, they are a joy.

The stone is often rather clinging and I find it easier to slice off wedges of the fruit by cutting down into the stone so that you have neat moon-shaped pieces to eat in a fruit salad or as an accompaniment to game or lamb. Leave the skin on.

GLOSSARY

PARMA HAM
This speciality of Italy is air-dried raw ham. It is usually sold cut wafer thin. Similar ham from Spain is called Serrano. Parma ham is traditionally served as a starter with fruit like melon or figs. Grated black pepper is essential as far as I am concerned.

PECTIN-CERTO, COMMERCIAL
You can buy this in chemists and most supermarkets when fruit for jam and marmalade is in season. The small bottle contains 250 ml (9 fl oz) of apple pectin extract which will set about 1 kg (2¼ lb) of fruit like strawberries, raspberries and blackberries. With fruit which sets easily like plums and gooseberries, the bottle would set about 1.8–2.25 kg (4–5 lb).

RELISH
Flavoured relishes, like chutneys, are based on fruit and/or vegetables. They usually contain sugar and vinegar but not in large enough quantities to preserve the ingredients for as long as most other pickles. The method of preparation of relishes is such that vegetables retain some of their crispness, through little or no cooking.

ROSEHIPS
In old recipes, rosehips must have been the quite small ones. Try to find the big fat red ones. It will be slightly less of a chore to de-seed them – but not much!

STEM GINGER IN SYRUP
This expensive preserve is bought most cheaply in wholefood shops. The peeled nuggets of ginger root are cooked in a sweet acid solution and the softened knobs then have brown sugar added which provides a milder sweet ginger in a delicious syrup. Its use is varied from eating after a meal to being chopped into a sweet sauce or cake icing. The syrup is often used to flavour cakes and biscuits or icing.

SUGAR, WARM
Do this easily in the microwave. Leave the exact weight of sugar in the paper bags and warm. Give the sugar 30 seconds. Increase by another 30 seconds or until the paper bag feels warm but not red hot.

INGREDIENTS INDEX

INGREDIENTS INDEX

INGREDIENTS INDEX

INGREDIENTS INDEX

Lemon
Juice used variously; lemons used as below:

Carrot & Lemon Jam 12
Lemon & Balsamic Vinegar Dressing 68
Lemon & Carrot Jam 11
Lemon Chutney 48
Lemons Preserved in Olive Oil 64
Microwave Seville Orange Marmalade 20
Miser's Minced Marmalade 21
Orange Gin 75
Preserved Lemon Wedges 64
Sweet & Sour Dressing Sauce 71
Tarragon & Lemon Jelly 18

Lettuce
Balsamic Dressing for Cos Lettuce 71

Lime
Juice used variously; limes used as below:

Apple Salsa 25
Avocado & Ginger Salsa 36
Beef Tomato Salsa 31
Guacamole Salsa 29
Lime & Ginger Marmalade 19
Miser's Minced Marmalade 21
Peanut Sauce 70
Sri Lankan Salsa 30

Lotus Root (see Radish)
Pickled Vegetables 61

Mango
Fresh Mango Relish 46
Mango Salad Salsa 26
Raita 68

Maple Syrup
Canadian Conserve with Apples
& Cranberries 14

Mascarpone
Grand Marnier & Mascarpone Sauce 70

Mayonnaise
Crunchy Peanut & Horseradish Dip 62
Garlic & Mayonnaise Dressing 72

Medlar
Magical Medlar Jelly 16

Mint
Mint & Coriander Fresh Relish 40
Mint & Elderberry Jelly 17
Mustard & Mint Salsa 29
Quick Mint Jelly in the Microwave 16

Mooli (White Radish)
Fresh Mint & Mooli Relish 47
Pickled Sugar 60
Pickled Vegetables 61
Ratatouille Chutney 50

Mustard
Dried Fruit & Mustard Relish 45
Hot Dog Mustard 62
Mustard & Dill Dip 62
Mustard & Mint Salsa 29

Nectarine
Low Sugar Nectarine (or Peach) Jam 11

Nuts (various)
Spiced Nuts 63

Olives
Charred Pepper Salsa 33
Minted Green Olives 59
Olives & Parma Ham 58
Olives & Red Pepper 58
Spicy Black Olives 59

Onion
Avocado & Coriander Salsa 33
Avocado & Ginger Salsa 36
Balsamic Pickled Onions 55
Beansprouts & Hot Peanut Sauce Salsa 35
Black Bean Salsa 28
Blackstrap Relish 46
Caribe Salsa 27
Chinese Dipping Sauce 61
Coconut Sambal 42
Cranberry Sweet & Sour Salsa 27
Cucumber Relish 38

INGREDIENTS INDEX

INGREDIENTS INDEX

ABOUT THE WI

If you have enjoyed this book, the chances are that you would enjoy belonging to the largest women's organisation in the country – the National Federation of Women's Institutes, or the WI as it is usually known.

We are friendly, go-ahead, like-minded women, who derive enormous satisfaction from all the movement has to offer. The list is long – you can make new friends, have fun and companionship, visit new places, develop new skills, take part in community services, fight local campaigns, become a WI Market producer, and play an active rôle in an organisation which has a national voice.

The WI is the only women's organisation in the country that owns an adult education establishment. At Denman College, you can take a course in anything from car maintenance to paper sculpture, from book binding to yoga, or cordon bleu cookery to fly fishing.

For more information, write to the **National Federation of Women's Institutes, 104 New Kings Road, London SW6 4LY, phone 0171-371-9300. The NFWI Wales Office is at 19 Cathedral Road, Cardiff CF1 9LJ, phone 01222-221712.**

PRESENTATION OF ITEMS FOR SHOWING

The Schedule: When entering a competition or show it is necessary to read the schedule carefully in order that the rules and instructions are fully understood. Many of the recipes in this book are <u>not true preserves</u> – ie. they are not intended to keep for several months. Some shows have a section for **Store Cupboard Items**, and many of the recipes may be suitable for exhibiting in this section.

Containers: Always make sure the foodstuff is exhibited in a suitable container with the appropriate cover or lid.

a) *Curds, Jams & Jellies*: a glass jar with a wax disc and cellophane cover.
b) *Jams & Jellies*: a glass jar with a twist top which has a plastic lining.
c) *Chutneys*: a glass jar with a vinegar-proof twist top.
d) *Other vinegar items*: a glass container with vinegar-proof tops.
e) *Foods in oil*: a glass container with plastic-lined twist tops or a cork.
f) *Jams, Jellies & Chutneys*: must be covered at a temperature above 82°C (180°F) to produce a seal.

Marking schemes: For detailed information refer to *On With the Show*, available from NFWI, 104 New Kings Road, London SW6 4LY.

ABOUT THE AUTHOR

GRACE MULLIGAN is probably best known as the presenter for 10 years of the long-running TV cookery programme *Farmhouse Kitchen*. The series, which actually ran for 20 years, was originally presented by another WI member, Dorothy Sleightholme, from Pickering, North Yorkshire.

A Home Economics teacher, Grace trained at the famous Edinburgh College of Domestic Science in Atholi Crescent and also at Moray House Teacher Training College in the Royal Mile. Grace comes from Dundee in the old county of Angus. It was after three years teaching in a large Secondary School in her home town that Grace married the medical student she had met in Edinburgh. They moved to Yorkshire to take up a job in General Practice. Despite having four children, Grace joined and became very involved in the newly formed Women's Institute in her village – Hook, near Goole, in the East Riding.

Along with a group of friends, Grace took part in the old proficiency exams after classes organised by the County Federation in Meal Cookery Preservation; Baking; Dressing Poultry; Staging; and Judging Eggs! Eventually they qualified as County Judges, and Grace and one other went on to become judges at National level. Grace was elected to the Executive Committee of the huge Yorkshire Federation. Eventually this led to work as a VCO, travelling the length and breadth of Yorkshire in all weathers. At this time, too, Grace was an invited member of the National Federation's Home Economics Committee under the chairmanship of Olive Odell in London.

It was through her work at the Great Yorkshire Show, at which the Yorkshire Federation put on a large exhibition, that Grace demonstrated cookery. The producer of *Farmhouse Kitchen* got in touch and invited Grace to take part in the programme on the ITV network. During all the years that the programme was made, many WI members took part. However, when Dorothy retired, it was she who nominated Grace to take her place.

Recipe writing followed – for the books published for the series. Grace contributed to some of the early books and eventually published under her own name. This she continues to do. She also contributes to several newspapers and magazines, including *Home & Country*. Her busy life consists of work with the Guild of Food Writers, travelling and also speaking engagements. One of her talks is called 'Travels with a Wooden Spoon'. Grace herself is amazed to find how much has happened to her just because of that wooden spoon.

TATE & LYLE SUGARS from cane to table

Tate & Lyle is the world's largest and Britain's only cane sugar refiner. It is also the UK's most popular sugar brand. Over the years, the company has received numerous letters from people who regularly make their own pickles and preserves, many of them attributing their successes to using only <u>cane</u> sugar – specifically Tate & Lyle.

A wide range of sugars, syrups and treacles are available, including two specialist sugars for preserving and conserving:

Tate & Lyle Jam Cane Sugar is high in pectin and is used with fruits such as strawberries and cherries which are naturally low in pectin. Using *Tate & Lyle Jam Cane Sugar* ensures that even inexperienced jam makers can produce a preserve that sets properly, without the need for long boiling or the addition of more sugar.

Preserving Cane Sugar contains much larger crystals and is ideal for making jams, jellies, marmalades and chutneys. The crystals dissolve slowly and retain enough space between them to prevent the sugar from settling in a dense layer on the bottom of the pan, so reducing the amount of stirring needed and preventing burning. Also, *Tate & Lyle Preserving Cane Sugar* produces less froth during boiling, so preserves will need less skimming and will be brighter and clearer.

The Secret of Sugar
Sugar acts as a natural preservative in a number of ways and is the key ingredient in a whole range of products. It is vital in jams, jellies and marmalades as it acts as the preservative agent, influences flavour and reacts with the acid and pectin in the fruit to obtain a set. If a jam is to keep well, the sugar should be 60-65% of the total finished weight of the jam.

When making preserves, if enough sugar is added, its highly water-attracting molecules take enough water out of circulation to allow the pectin molecules in the fruit to reach each other, causing them to form a firm network. In this mesh-like structure, large amounts of water can be held.

Tate & Lyle Preserving Cane Sugar and *Jam Cane Sugar* are the most convenient to use and produce the clearest, most sparkling preserves. They do not cause the formation of froth, minimising the skimming necessary, and the finished preserve is brighter and clearer.

For recipe ideas, further details about Tate & Lyle cane products, or advice with any preserving or jam making problems, please contact the **Tate & Lyle Information Service, Althorp Studios, 4-6 Althorp Road, Wandsworth Common, London SW17 7ED, or telephone 0181-682-1633.**